W9-CMJ-825

ST. MARY'S CITY, MARYLAND 20686

The Wearing of Costume

THE WEARING of COSTUME

*The Changing Techniques of Wearing
Clothes and How to Move in Them
From Roman Britain to the
Second World War*

RUTH M. GREEN

DRAMA PUBLISHERS
NEW YORK

First Drama Publishers edition 1995

All rights reserved. No part of this book may be reproduced in any form or by any means without permission in writing from the publishers. For information address Drama Publishers, 260 Fifth Avenue, New York, NY 10001.

Green, Ruth M.
    The wearing of costume: the changing techniques of wearing clothes and how to move in them, from Roman Britain to the Second World War / Ruth M. Green.
       p. cm.
    Originally published: London: Pitman, 1966.
    Includes index.
    ISBN 0-89676-141-X
    1. Costume—Great Britain—History. I. Title:
GT730.G7   1995   95–25662
391′.00941—dc20   CIP

© 1966 Ruth M. Green

To C. H. Gibbs-Smith
to whose encouragement I owe so much

Preface

"MANNERS makyth man." They say the cowl does not make the monk, but if he wears it in the right manner he will seem much more a monk. So, taking the clothes for granted, it is the manner of wearing them that I am concerned with here.

There are many books on costume. Their authors claim, with some justification, that because of them historic personages, real and imaginary, are now generally imagined and presented in more or less accurate dress. When this happens their credibility and reality is somehow enhanced. I don't know why this is, but even for people ignorant of these things there is an instinctive reaction to the difference between fancy dress and a near-documentary showing of the truth.

That is where this book comes in, for when you have a fine tool you need to know how to use it. The most correct costume looks like fancy dress if you don't know how to wear it, and when you do know you'll find the clothes give more scope than you thought. So I am writing for two sets of people. For the readers of history (and of historical novels), to round out the pictures and people seen in their minds' eye; and for the actors and producers who would re-create these people "in their habits as they lived," since you can use a stage technique to create an effect only after you know what effect you need. (Judging by much we see on stage and screen, this part of the actor's technique is taught inadequately if at all.)

Because it is easier to understand things in terms of oneself I shall write as though for a person who intends to wear the clothes. That way the reader will get a clearer picture of what was done, and understand the reasons for it. The dates that are mentioned are approximate guides, not to be taken too precisely. People do not change their habits or their fashions overnight.

Except for the drawings reproduced from *Punch*, all the illustrations in this book were specially drawn by Miss Zena Flax from contemporary sources, which have been named when the provenance seemed particularly interesting. They should not be taken as guides to fashion, however, since they have been deliberately simplified; their function being to illustrate how the clothes were worn, ornaments and other distracting details have been ignored.

I should like to express my thanks to the staffs of the Victoria and Albert Museum, the British Museum, and the Wallace Collection, and to many librarians (whose names I never learnt) for their constant helpfulness. My thanks are also due to *Punch* for permission to reproduce parts of twelve drawings.

RUTH M. GREEN

Contents

PART I
Basic Principles

Chapter 1

The General Background

Naturally no two people move in the same way—personal character, general circumstances, the immediate situation, all cause variations. These subtleties I leave each person to work out for himself. We are concerned with the broad outline, the general ideal, the "main road" which all the personal idiosyncrasies spring from. The greatest unconventionality can exist only in contrast to a corresponding convention. So remember that a man's manner and behaviour will be coloured by his social position, to name just one thing, and allow the appropriate modifications.

Let us begin with the basic principles that have never changed.

First, *people live in their clothes*. Whatever they wear, people always find the least troublesome way of managing their clothes. So if you do as the original wearers did you will have far more freedom in your clothes. But people have always been concerned with more than ease and comfort. They want to look as attractive as possible according to the ideas of their time; to show off their clothes to the best advantage; and most people conform to current ideas of propriety. (However convenient it may be to lift your skirt above your waist, if it is generally considered indecent you won't do it in public.) The weight, shape and stiffness or otherwise of your clothes—including underclothes—

3

affects your posture and balance; so you must always know what people wore under their clothes (e.g. corsets) before you can tell how they moved. And lastly, custom and childhood training leave a mark. Hours of schooldays spent practising deportment or wearing a backboard have a permanent effect, as easily recognizable as the gait of a soldier or sailor.

It may be objected that I concentrate too much on the manners and attire of the rich and noble. This is of course deliberate, since they always showed more nicety in both; also, in this case the richer largely includes the poorer. The very poor could not waste time or money or energy on refinements. Those with more of each aped the classes above them, as witness the sumptuary laws of Elizabeth I. So if we know what the aristocracy did we know what the middle classes were trying to copy, although they might well be behind the times, still aiming at old fashions. But these things need practice. It was not only snobbishness that made people laugh at a dressed-up servant girl, for instance. Put a girl into a crinoline for the first time, or gird a sword on a modern young man, and their efforts to control them will be genuinely funny. You try it.

Servants are usually, at least in front of their "betters," less flamboyant and move quietly. But it is important to remember that the idea that serving another person is lowering and undignified is a strictly modern one. Until recently a man or woman could take as much pride in being a good servant—which does not mean being servile— as in any other skill. Just as the good master did not merely use other people but felt a responsibility to his "family." That is not to say there were no rebellious or ambitious servants before this century, but that this was the climate of opinion.

The middle classes, on the whole, are always inclined to be quietly correct and less flamboyant than the others, however intransigent they may be politically. They are the stronghold of propriety, taking trouble always to maintain a sober decency in dress and manner, and avoiding extremes.

Ideas of propriety change. Until less than a hundred years ago it was proper for all women but the young un-married ones to wear some kind of head covering. Until the seventeenth century no woman exposed any part of her arm, however low her neckline (unless she was in a state of undress, or like a washerwoman engaged on work that required it). Then sleeves crept up to the elbow and stayed elbow-length—never higher—until the end of the eighteenth century. Then, when it was the fashion to wear flimsy dresses that entirely revealed the shape they covered, sleeves rose higher and the whole arm was bared. In the nineteenth century, while day dresses had long sleeves, evening dresses bared the arm; this was one of the charac-teristics of evening dress. The custom of dressing for dinner was followed, until the Second World War, by anyone with pretensions to social position. In the nineteen-twenties it was again correct to bare the whole arm at any time of day. Now fashion varies the smart length of women's sleeves every few years (though evening dresses, even when high-necked, are usually sleeveless); decency and propriety have nothing to do with it.

With men the story is different. At different times they have shown the shape of their legs, arms and bodies in tight-fitting clothes. But they never actually bared any part, unless you count as doing this the loose Byronic collar or today's open-necked, short-sleeved sports shirts, which are still strictly for informal wear. At times, however, they have had to learn to live with women whose clothes got in their companions' way. For instance, when women wore large hoops it became second nature for men not to attempt to come too close to them—the result could be embarrassing. Similarly when smart dresses had trains in the late nineteenth century men automatically allowed for them, so the ladies were not forever bothered about their trains being walked on.

Such things did sometimes happen, of course, but they were the exception and not the rule. In this way men and women have always made unconscious allowances for each other.

Because the changes in women's clothes have usually been more violent and complete there will be more to say about managing their clothes than men's. Men's clothes have always allowed more freedom, but in one thing at least men must be more careful than women. Until comparatively recently, when loose trousers came in, the shape of a man's legs has been visible. So the slight sagging at the knee, which most modern men get away with, was not previously allowable except for the old, the ill or the scared. In tight hose or knee breeches it was appallingly obvious. Even in today's clothes a man will find his whole appearance improved if he straightens his knees. Remember, a good leg has always been an asset. Everyone knows that an actor in eighteenth-century costume places his white-stockinged legs as "stylishly" an he can. How many, even of the actors, know that this is in order to show them off as one of his manly charms? Today it is the girl with good legs who shows them off. It used, without any affectation, to be the man; they were a recognized sexual attraction, like his lady's small waist. This fact, often unconsciously, affected their placing. Look at any eighteenth-century painting of a ball or assembly and you'll see how the men are showing themselves off as a matter of course.

You will notice too that their feet are often in one or other of the basic ballet positions—the comfortable third position is particularly popular. This is not surprising, since ballet evolved from the masques performed for, and by, the aristocracy—the French kings of the seventeenth century were proud of their performances in the early ballets. The fashion of turned-out toes lasted so very long that it can hardly be called a fashion. Starting with seventeenth-century men it continued through the eighteenth century (when ballet started to evolve into what it is today). In the late nineteenth century Alice in Wonderland was still taught to turn out her toes. She was taught this at the dancing class which every well brought-up child attended, both boys and girls. Well into this century schoolchildren were being taught to stand with heels together and toes turned out.

Another thing men must remember is the evolution of the court bow. In the Middle Ages a man went straight down with the weight forward, as in a woman's curtsey; at the deepest he was more or less kneeling on one knee. As the years passed the bow changed, with the man's weight shifting farther back and his body bending forward, until in the eighteenth century his weight was thrown entirely on the back foot while the other pointed prettily forward and his body bent toward it. At the same time he took off his hat and either held it before his heart, held it behind him with his arm parallel to his body, or took it through the first position into the second in one elaborate movement. A well performed bow showed off a man's leg so well that it was often referred to as "making a leg." Be careful to suit your bow to your clothes and their period.

Remember that you cannot learn to move, to bow or to manage a hoop, sword, spurs, ruffles, etc., simply by reading about it. Learn the theory, then practise it. An actor can and should rehearse in practice clothes, a canvas-covered hoop is more use at this stage than the ball dress the audience will see. Make a skirt or a train from an old sheet, get used to a weight on your head if you're going to wear a wig, push a stick in your belt to remind you to allow for the sweep of a sword. Study the theory in this book first, manage things correctly, and with practice they'll soon be no trouble. But it you don't consider them until the last moment—oh dear!

1. Note how casually she lifts her skirt, as though hardly conscious of what she is doing—actually she is showing off her underskirt.

Chapter 2

The Management of Long Skirts

WALKING IN A LONG SKIRT

THE long skirt is a regular hazard for the modern woman. She doesn't know how to walk in it and is forever lifting it (usually clumsily) so that her hands are never free. If you walk properly it need only be lifted to get it out of the dirt and to mount stairs. Though the latter should not always be necessary; a lady who was young in the last century once told me that she was made to practise walking in a skirt several inches too long for her. Her teacher was not satisfied until she could walk *upstairs* in it without using her hands! After that she was at ease in anything. If you are not used to it your feet can tie knots in the material; yet all you need do is let your foot push the skirt forward, away from you, at the end of each step. You must take comparatively small steps for two reasons: first because too large a stride will make you lose your balance, and second because it is both ugly and unladylike, at any date.

You want a smooth forward flow of your skirt moving together with your whole body. None of Herrick's "Tempestuous petticoat," which he equated with untied shoe laces. Walk from the knee. When you turn, move your whole body in a single clean movement, moving your feet

2. c. 1500. The lady holds her very long, heavy and voluminous skirt with her arm, both keeping it out of the dirt and moving more freely. Note that the exposed underskirt reaches her instep, but she has no need to lift it.

at the same time so that everything turns together in a big neat movement. This is a good basis for style, and a frequent ingredient in the "grand manner."

Be sure of the length of your skirt. If it covers your foot and touches the floor you must keep it moving with you. If it rests on your instep when you hold yourself upright there is no need to push it. You still need to move smoothly with smallish steps, but the forward push of the foot, if visible and therefore unnecessary, looks silly. In fact you should never poke your foot far forward out of your skirt. At most, the tip of your toe should show.

LIFTING A LONG SKIRT

This should never be done unless it is absolutely necessary— and that is not often if you move properly in your clothes. Sometimes, of course, the skirt was deliberately lifted to show off the underskirt as in Drawing 1. The precise method varies according to the dress. For instance, the excessively long and full skirts of the fourteenth and fifteenth centuries are held unlike any others. Take as much fullness as possible to the centre front and lift it high, at least to your waist, showing the handsome petticoat beneath. You take more fullness than your hand can easily hold, because you can hold it against you with your arm (see Drawings 2 and 38); and you can use both arms for this as in Drawing 39. Another way of raising this skirt is to hang the extra fullness over one arm (see Drawing 3). When these skirts grew excessive in length, voluminousness and weight this was a less convenient way of holding them, one more used by the bourgeoisie than by the great lady. It is permissible to hold these skirts breast high or even to your chin, although this is a little extreme. It was fashionable at that time to have a slightly pregnant look.

In the eighteen-nineties and nineteen-hundreds there was also a distinctive way of holding up your skirt. You only

3. Fourteenth century. This young girl carries her extremely long, full skirt over her arm. Note that although her underskirt trails on the ground she does not need to lift it.

need one hand for this; gather all the fullness you can to one side, a little to the back (see Drawings 4, 5 and 89). This is an amazingly convenient way to handle those full but not trailing skirts. It looks very effective too. Your skirts will be shortest immediately below your hand; remember that to show two inches of leg above your ankles is *not nice*. An old lady I know who was young and "in service" in those days once showed two inches of leg by accident. It was a wet, muddy day and she was only thinking of keeping the hem of her skirt out of the dirt as she hurried home. Her father happened to see her, and in 1960 she told me she still remembered the scolding he gave her!

For most periods, however, the correct way to lift your skirt is as follows. Let your arms hang easily, just in front of your thighs. Take hold of the material lying under your fingers and, by slightly raising your hands and bending your elbows, the whole front of your skirt is lifted in a quiet, unobtrusive and well-bred manner. A very small movement will clear your path. If you have only one hand free the action is the same but you must place your hand more centrally, spread your fingers to grasp more material and raise your hand higher to get the same clearance. Remember that the movement of hands and arms should be as small and unaccentuated as possible. You are performing an action as ordinary as turning a door handle; to make a fuss about it shows you up as a poor creature unused to such clothes (or else decidedly vulgar). Incidentally, this is the way to handle a modern long evening dress. The habit of sewing a loop to the train of a dress, to lift it by when dancing, came from the change in the general style of ballroom dancing with the popularity of the waltz.

OPEN-FRONTED SKIRTS (SIXTEENTH CENTURY)

For over a century it was fashionable for ladies to leave an open panel in the front of their skirts, showing a rich

4. Late nineteenth century. A Dana Gibson lady, in evening dress. Holding it like this she will walk up or down stairs and sit down at table with no trouble. Note that it has not occurred to her to *lift* her skirt, only to control it.

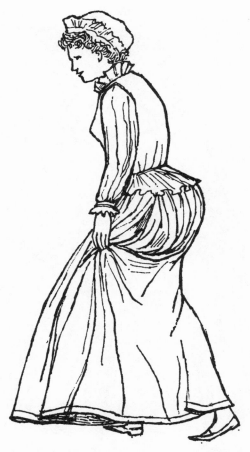

5. Late nineteenth century. A respectable low-class woman handles her skirt in the same way as a great lady. Note that she too is concerned with controlling it, not with lifting it.

6. End of the sixteenth century. Her hands rest against the widest part of her farthingale, in which apparently restful position she can control it.

underskirt. This dress, should, when necessary, be lifted in the way just described. But be careful! Take hold simultaneously of both the overdress and the skirt beneath, so that they stay in the *same relation to each other*. If you stop to think, this is common sense. To lift the outer skirt only makes no practical difference. Lift the underskirt only, then the other will trail and balloon behind you; and, what is worse, you will probably betray yourself. For the underskirt was rarely as rich as it seemed; often only the panel that showed was fine, while the rest was of poorer, plainer, coarser stuff. This is nearly always the case in modern stage costumes; in fact they sometimes have no more than a contrasting panel in a single skirt, which gives the right impression at a distance. By only lifting "one" skirt you'll give away the secret; lift both skirts and your secret is safe.

HOOPS

Hoops are a case apart. Three separate times they have been in fashion. There was the sixteenth-century farthingale, the eighteenth-century hoop, and the nineteenth-century crinoline. They were not identical and cannot be treated in quite the same way but they have much in common, particularly the two last. You will always be correct with hands clasped loosely in front of you, but with all of them it is comfortable to let your hands rest lightly on the swell of the skirt (see Drawings 6, 42, 43, 62 and 63). In this way you can control it, hold it still and guide it a little. Remember that a hooped skirt, though large, is less static than any other. The slightest movement, particularly of the hips, sets your skirts swinging. So you must move smoothly, with small steps, keeping your hips steady so that it never swings far unchecked in any direction. If it does, or if you want to turn sharply, your hands are ready to guide and control. The important thing is to move *smoothly*; you'll seem to float.

7. 1669. The lady sits correctly, with her knees wide apart.

If you move badly in hoop or crinoline an indecent amount of legs and underclothes shows. (It was not until the nineteenth century that ladies wore drawers.) You could get a lot of fun and excitement out of those constantly quivering skirts that any moment might expose your petticoats, or more. Eighteenth-century men sometimes claimed to have seen the colour of a lady's garters! In the theatre I am always surprised to see how little use is made of this aspect of hoops; only think what scope it gives for hoydens and fast women.

TRAINED SKIRTS

You may need to move backwards in a long skirt, or wearing a train. Impossible to lift it out of the way and still be decent; *perhaps* you might use your hands to draw it back, away from your heels, but this is difficult and not necessary. Simply *keep your feet on the ground*. Take small, smooth steps, sliding your feet back so that your heels push the folds of cloth away. By keeping your feet on the ground you avoid the danger of treading on your skirt. Be careful to keep your balance; you'll probably find it easier if you take smaller steps than when walking forward. This is a manœuvre that requires a lot of practice. It is amazingly simple in itself, yet if you don't do it properly it is so easy to totter and stumble. The showy method of kicking your train out of your way is fairly modern and has a touch of vulgarity. Almost the only justification is if you have to make a quick, sharp turn and haven't enough room.

One of the more effective and picturesque uses of a train is to have it lying swirled across your feet as you sit or stand. (Drawing 36 is an example of this; it was popular in the late nineteenth century when smart dresses had a short train.) It makes a charming picture and incidentally keeps the train under your eye, where no one is likely to tread on it by accident. It is quite easy to achieve without using your

8. Eighteenth century. A lady sitting quietly at home. Note how she sits with her knees apart, and that she wears a cap with lappets hanging down her back.

hands at all, in fact you cannot do it at all easily with your hands; what it needs is forethought. Having decided where your train will finally lie, walk past the spot you mean to stand on so that the train is in the right position; then make a half-turn *into* it. If you work it out properly beforehand, and move with the right casual air, you not only get the effect you want but it seems almost accidental, as though your skirt did it by itself. It sounds complicated, but a little practice will make it quite easy. Let me give one warning. If you sit with the train of your skirt disposed in this manner make sure you are not accidentally treading on a fold of it before you stand up.

One last generalization about ladies' skirts: be sure you wear enough petticoats. A safe *minimum* is three, but you can wear more. With less your dress won't hang at all well. It will either seem skimpy, or show the lines of the body beneath too clearly, or look floppy and poor. Literally poor; as though you can't afford to dress decently.

And, ladies, never, never cross your legs except in strictest privacy. That, like our careless slouching and lolling, is a very modern habit. It used to be improper. It was usual for ladies to sit with their knees apart, making a broad lap (see Drawings 7, 8 and 58). We don't do that now; it isn't nice with our short skirts.

The long-skirted countrywoman who needed, or liked, to walk a great deal doubtless developed a longer, more swinging step for this purpose—how else could Emily Brontë, for example, have taken and enjoyed her long walks on the moors? But she would try to walk differently in polite society. This was the kind of thing that gave added point to the gibes at "country gentlewomen" in Restoration comedies. It is another way in which your manner betrays the life you lead.

9. Saxon. Centre-fastened cloak. He has pulled it forward so
that his upper body is covered, yet his arms are unimpeded.

Chapter 3

Cloaks

CLOAKS were a routine part of everyone's wardrobe for a very long time. On the whole women have worn them less than men—they rang the changes with mantles, stoles, tippets, shawls. Now, of course, we all wear coats, which fit in the same way as our other garments. There was a time—late Medieval, early Renaissance—when a man could use his gown as an extra garment. But it was a garment that went with position, seniority, age, as much as with the temperature; the cloak was still worn. In the time of Elizabeth I, when men's fashions changed as fast as women's now, there were many styles of cloak. The basic rules for wearing them are the same for both sexes. Master these, and you can find many variations of your own. The precise manner of wearing a cloak was a very personal thing. On the whole men had more scope than women because they did not have to drape it over such voluminous garments.

In the days of the Saxons and the Normans cloaks were fastened with a brooch, either in the centre of the breast (as in Drawings 9 and 10) or on the right shoulder (as in Drawings 11 and 12). The latter method left the right arm free, and you could always fold the cloak back over the left arm. Later, cloaks were tied on; once fastened firmly they could be draped as you pleased. But the mechanics

10. Eleventh century (Bayeux tapestry). Centre-fastened cloak, worn a little differently from that of the man in Drawing 9.

11. Eleventh century (Bayeux tapestry). His cloak is fastened on the right shoulder, leaving that arm completely free. Note that its fullness is pulled forward so that there is no drag on his left arm.

12. Eleventh century (Bayeux tapestry). Duke William sits in state. Note how, with his cloak fastened on the right shoulder, he has pulled much of the fullness forward (right down on his lap).

of the thing insist that the cloak must come over at least one shoulder. Theatrical costumiers sometimes provide a short cloak fastened to the shoulder blades, presumably intended for trimming. If it were correctly tied on a man wearing it in that position he would be half choked, and would never be able to pull it round him if he needed to. This foolishness usually applies especially to the short Elizabethan cloak; but that was still basically functional (see Drawings 13, 14 and 48).

The Medieval man, whose cloak was a large piece of cloth he might want to take with him but not wear, had evolved a neat way to do this. He folded it into a long rectangle and threw it across one shoulder.

Drawings 15–22 are typical examples of how the great cloak could be worn. The man and woman of Drawings 15 and 16 have wrapped it right round themselves, apparently for warmth, and she has brought it up to cover her head as well. In Drawings 17–19 the great cloak and a loose outer gown have been treated in the same way, being drawn across the knees while sitting (the Prioress is actually riding, but the same thing applies). This is both comfortable and an easy way of disposing of the great folds of material. The gentlemen in Drawings 20–22 have each found a different way, convenient and comfortable, of wearing their cloaks.

Cloaks were often lined, and their wearers might then fold or drape them so as to show off the lining. Think, for instance, of a fur-lined cloak fastened on the right shoulder with the opposite edge turned up to lie on the left shoulder. The effect on a man's appearance, the implications about his wealth and his taste, are considerable, not to mention his own ease of movement.

There are an infinite number of ways of wearing the garment, and everyone worked out those that suited him best. The way a cloak is worn can indicate both the type of person the wearer is and his present condition—modest, secretive, vain, hot, cold, etc.

13. Elizabethan gentleman. His fashionable cloak is well over one shoulder although it has begun to slip off the other. Note the hand casually resting on the sword hilt.

In practice, remember that a cloak bellies like a sail with the wind of your movement, and allow for this. You may sometimes even make this happen deliberately. Remember too, when flinging your cloak firmly about you, to see that it does not knock anything over—or catch on something else—in the process.

14. This sixteenth century gentleman has pulled his cloak well over one shoulder.

15. Fourteenth century. One way of wrapping a cloak about you. A modern person would tend to place the actual wrapover higher, since ideas of good proportion change.

16. Fourteenth century woman. She has wrapped her cloak about her like the man in Drawing 15, but with certain differences. It is drawn up over her head, wrapped closely around her left arm, and drawn across her body higher. She has created a more feminine effect with the same garment.

17. Late twelfth century. The cloak is pulled well over one shoulder and then lapped across the knees, which is both warm and convenient. The whole garment is used; there is no spare fullness to get in the way or need careful management. Note how it is turned back at shoulder and knee to show the fur lining.

18. Fourteenth century. Chaucer's Prioress (Ellesmere Manuscript). She has drawn her gown over her knee like the king in Drawing 17 and for the same reason. Note how the "extra" length is used to cover her feet.

19. Fifteenth century. He has drawn his gown across his knees too. Note that he has turned it back at knee and shoulder to show the lining.

20. Early fifteenth century. He has draped his cloak right round him and flung the end over his right shoulder, out of the way.

21. 1689. The cloak keeps his face warm, and he has a muff for
his hands.

22. Another convenient way to wear a cloak.

Chapter 4

Shirts—Covered Heads— Pockets—Shoes

SHIRTS

A GENTLEMAN could wear a cloak or not, according to his mood. But the rule about not appearing in his shirt sleeves did not change until the middle of this century. It was simply not done in public—except by a poor man with literally no other upper garment, or perhaps a labourer on a hot day, or a man under great emotional shock and strain. There is a fashion in the theatre for showing gentlemen in their shirt sleeves whenever possible. But only an eccentric was likely to stay long in this condition, even in private. Correct wear for fencing, fighting or sports was a case apart, but only a boor would have appeared before ladies in his shirt.

Immediately after the Restoration a lot of shirt was shown, but not the whole shirt. In the nineteenth century the shirt *front* was seen. Otherwise only the wrist ends of the sleeves and a small area near the throat showed. It was essentially an undergarment, and it is only very recently that shirts have become outer garments in their own right.

A servant would never appear on duty in his shirt sleeves. Countrymen at work, ignoring fashions and having no

tailor to cut them coats, covered their shirts with the
traditional smock for warmth and decency. This was
still worn in some remote country districts after the mid-
nineteenth century.

A curious theatrical fashion of wearing a shirt without an
outer garment is often used in performances of Elizabethan
plays. Here the idea is probably reinforced by the singular
contemporary picture of a romantic young man in his shirt,
but the young man was showing his peculiar state by his
dress, or lack of it. The phrase "In his shirt" meant a man
who had had no time to dress, or was too mad to want to.
For easy wear there was the gown which, if fastened, hid the
absence of a stiff doublet underneath.

COVERED HEADS

The greatest difference in women's manners between
previous ages and our own is that women of all classes
always covered their heads. Unmarried girls might wear
their hair loose, but nobody else. Until the middle of the
twelfth century it was common to have thick plaits, bound
with ribbon, falling below the wimple. Later no hair
was shown at all. Centuries later still it could be glimpsed
through gauze or elaborate nets, but in England women's
hair (all but the youngest) was covered until the days of the
Tudors. It is still accepted as a poetical cliché that a woman
so distraught and abandoned to grief that she is beyond
caring about anything else has her hair loose. In the days
when English thought was taking shape this really meant a
lot. For even the poorest girl, whose skirts were short for
fieldwork, covered her hair. The barefoot shepherdess of
Drawing 24 is such a girl; like every Medieval and early
Renaissance woman, no matter what class she belonged
to, this shepherdess conforms to the canons of decency;
she has no hair showing at all.

POCKETS

Through most of history women's dresses have had no pockets as we know them, but there was no need to fumble for a place to keep small objects. In the Middle Ages and after—until quite recently, in fact—pockets were slung on a waistband and worn *under* the skirt; you could wear either

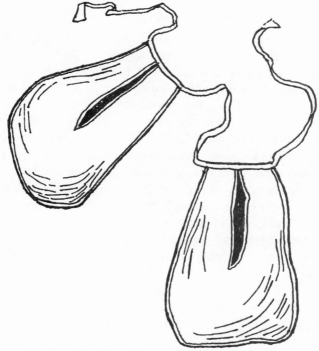

23. A pair of pockets, to be worn under the skirt.

one or two, as in Drawing 23. Readers of *Adam Bede* will remember how three-year-old Totty "with great gravity lifted up her frock and showed a tiny pink pocket."

You usually reached your pocket through a slit in your skirt. Dean Swift, in a monologue entitled *Mrs Frances Harris's Petition* makes the lady's maid explain how she keeps her money "in my pocket, ty'd about my middle, next my smock," and how "When I went to put up my purse, my smock was unript, And instead of putting it into my pocket, down it slipt." But in general such a pocket was a very safe place. In fact, in the earlier part of this century a shop-keeper I knew still used just such a pocket for safety while in the shop.

SHOES

Until the late sixteenth century heels were never worn. Shoes varied from crude coverings for the feet to veritable works of art in dyed leather and fine cloths. When shoes were made of delicate stuff and worn in strange, fashionable shapes they needed protection from mud and dirt, so what developed into the patten was worn by both sexes out of doors. This was basically a thick wooden sole with a ring or strap through which to put the shod foot. Pattens were worn for centuries, and must have affected the gait of anyone wearing them. Steps become jerkier, probably shorter, and certainly noisy. Practice might enable you to walk tolerably fast in pattens, but I doubt if you could run in them. Figure 25 shows one each of the two pairs of pattens that are lying about the room in Van Eyck's famous portrait of Arnolfini and his wife in the National Gallery. Presumably one pair was his and the other hers. There were, of course, many types of patten, of varying heights, but the general idea, like the function, was the same.

Mrs. Gamp was still using pattens, in the middle of the nineteenth century; but by then they were only worn by the unfashionable poor.

Chapter 5

Children

CHILDREN have always had to know as much about the techniques of wearing clothes as adults did, since during most of history they have worn similar clothes to their parents, with all the inconvenience of swords, stays and hoops. The only exception to this was in the first five or six years of boys' lives. Until well into the last century small boys wore petticoats, and a boy's "breeching" was often quite a ceremony.

Children's clothes first had a style of their own in the late eighteenth century, with Kate Greenaway type dresses for girls and Little Boy Blue outfits (not necessarily blue) for boys. In the nineteenth century all but very young girls followed adult styles again, although they were allowed much shorter skirts than their mothers wore. Age showed more in hair-styles, and putting up her hair was as important to a girl in her teens as his breeching ever was to a boy. It was the sign of being grown-up. In the twentieth century children have had their own, constantly changing fashions, clothes which have little to do with adult fashions and require no skill in their wearers—but since the First World War, of course, adult clothes have been easier to wear too.

In most respects children were as adept at managing the clothes of any period as their parents. There were minor differences of course, but the greatest difference is always that children care less about current ideas of propriety.

PART II
Changing Manners

Chapter 6

Antiquity

THE people of Roman Britain wore Roman dress which was, basically, tunics of varying lengths and cloaks. Pre-Roman Britain, as far as we know, had the same basic wardrobe, and men may have worn breeches. Legend describes Boadicea as wearing a loose dress or tunic, with a cloak fastened by a brooch. However, this book is not a history of costume but of how people wore their clothes.

These clothes were not at all constricting. Only the toga might be called that in some degree; yet properly draped it was comfortable to wear and, because of its symbolic meaning, it was worn with pride (it was the garb of a Roman Citizen). The main difference in attitude between then and later was that pagans could be proud of their bodies. It is true that women wore long skirts and a long tunic on a man would be a sign of age or eminence, and they had definite ideas about decent behaviour; but they did not suffer from the conviction of many Medieval Christians that the human body is almost automatically an enticement to sin. The shamefastness inculcated by this was missing; which does not mean that they were immodest, but that their modesty had a different quality.

There are certain points which an actor playing a Roman or a Romanized Celt should remember. The Roman legions had their own particular marching step, that carried them

47

through an eight-hour day on the march. (Even today the armies of different countries differ in their ways of marching.) Clothes varied with position in society; for instance, when a boy came of age he wore a different toga, the toga virilis.

This was a slave economy, and the demeanour of a born slave was surely different from that of one who had been taken prisoner and made a slave when fully grown. And whatever a slave's attitude to life was, it must have been different from that of free men. Again, a freedman would have a different attitude from that of people born free. Strangely, I have found very few references to freedwomen, although there must have been a good many of them; there were certainly plenty of female slaves.

All these differences among slaves and free were subtle things, but they were based on more definite inequalities between people than any of our class distinctions today, or even a century ago.

Chapter 7

The Dark Ages
and The Middle Ages

In the Dark Ages and the Middle Ages what we call comfort hardly existed—no draughtless rooms, for instance, and very little privacy—and there was little subtlety in dress or in the manner of wearing it. It was a time of heavy, flowing draperies for those who could afford them—still basically the belted tunic and cloak. The rich and lordly who wanted to wear gold and jewels had them in the shape of neck chains, brooches, rings and girdles. There were also circlets for the head. Arm rings were for men, rather than women; in the clothes of the time with long, full sleeves there was no point in a woman wearing bracelets, while old tales make it clear that the Vikings, at least, wore gold arm rings, when they could get them. Finger rings could be worn on any finger, including the thumb.

Villeins and serfs wore what they could get and had no time to care how they wore it, beyond the requirements of basic decency. Constant hard work, exposure to all weathers, and lack of care doubtless aged them early.

It was a time when all classes wore clothes of similar style and shape, yet you could quickly tell a man's class by his clothes and manner—feudal society was very clear cut and everyone had his own place in it, which he usually accepted.

RELIGIOUS

Monks, of course, were marked by the very different life they led. The age at which a man first entered the monastic life showed in his manner. He who joined an Order in middle age after an active life would keep some signs of earlier days, quite unconsciously; while he who had been an oblationary child and grown up in the monastic life would be quieter and gentler in demeanour, however bold his spirit. The difference would show in small things such as a bigger stride, a bolder glance, and probably louder and more impetuous speech.

Nuns were expected to behave with the usual female propriety, but carried further than in other women.

Certain decencies of behaviour were expected of religious of both sexes, in public, although the ideal was not always achieved, of course. Their movements were smaller and quieter; they were expected not to fidget, and not to let their eyes wander all over the place, but to keep hands composed and quiet, eyes low and still. Remember, there was more security in their lives than in anyone else's, in spite of all scandals and upsets. It was bound to show in their demeanour.

THE LAITY

MEN

Every properly brought-up nobleman went through the degrees of page and squire in the same way that a craftsman was apprenticed, so that he knew what was correct behaviour even if he chose to ignore it. And deliberate bad manners have a quite different quality from ignorant bad manners. He was used to arms and armour, which is heavy and bound to make one move a bit clumsily, with big, heavy steps and gestures. Such things mark a man, even in "civilian" clothes.

A man's tunic, even when full length, cleared the ground, and later it had one or more slits in it, too; so his free stride was not impeded. The scrip or purse he wore fastened to his belt was usually at the side, sometimes in front. They were still worn, centuries later, by the men in Drawings 32 and 33.

Women's clothes at this time were not constricting in any way. The idea was to hide the figure rather than to show it off. So your arms lie easily, straight at your sides following the unbroken line of your gown, and your movements do not draw attention to your shape—in theory that is, and usually in practice. (But not always, or there would not have been so many sermons against it. Who can imagine Henry II's beautiful Queen Eleanor minimizing her charms in any way?)

You should not "walk mannishly" but should keep your steps rather small. You cannot lift your skirt very high as your stockings end below the knee, where they are gartered.

Women wore no underclothes in our sense of the word, but several layers of similarly shaped garments. It was usual to wear at least two, a dress over a linen shift. To protect the outer dress from the dirt of a working day you kilted it up over the undergarments; this seems to have been more common than the wearing of any type of apron. The poor shepherdess and well-to-do miller's wife of Drawings 24 and 26 are early fifteenth-century women whose tight sleeves and figure-fitting dresses would have been improper, even shocking, in earlier centuries; but in this they are typical of their predecessors. The barefooted girl with her short shift has kilted her skirt high, as far out of the way as she can get it; probably it is her only dress. Anyway, her work takes her away from disapproving eyes so she can afford to be more concerned with protecting her dress than with maidenly modesty. However dirty her shift gets, when she goes back to the village she can drop her clean skirt over it and look respectable.

24. Second quarter of the fifteenth century (Devonshire tapestries). The shepherdess has her hair carefully covered. Her skirt is kilted high over her smock, to keep it clean.

The miller's wife also wants to keep her dress clean, but she has kilted her skirt very differently. It is not raised at all at the back, and not raised nearly so high in front. In fact she has raised it as little as she can if she is to hope to keep it clean (she must have a servant to do the dirtiest work). She too, when she wants to look her smartest, will

25. Pattens—one each from different pairs. There were many styles of patten, but they all fulfilled the same function.

drop a clean skirt over a dirtied petticoat. Note that, even with her skirt raised, this respectable woman's legs are properly covered.

See how, even in such a casual thing as the kilting of a skirt, they tell us a lot about themselves—their social position, the sort of work they do or have done for them, how much they bother about what a casual passer-by may think of them, how conventional they are or can afford to be. This is a small example of how the wearing of clothes within the conventions of a period, in fact *using* them, is a sharp-edged and flexible tool for showing a person's character,

26. Second quarter of the fifteenth century (Devonshire tapestries). The miller's wife has more elaborate headgear. Her skirt is kilted too, showing underskirt, shoes and thick stockings. As some modern women knit, she plies her distaff, not wasting a moment.

situation, etc. (Both the women have every scrap of hair covered, for that was a matter of decency rather than convention.)

MEN

Thirteenth and Fourteenth Centuries. At the end of the thirteenth century styles changed. There were exciting, new and lovely materials to use, and new styles came in. From now on the idea was to show off your figure under your clothes, and there was altogether less bulkiness. This particularly applied to men. Their clothes fitted closely to the figure, with tight-fitting sleeves, and gay young men often showed the whole length of their legs, the effect being similar to that of a ballet dancer's tights. These are clothes that show the beauty—and flaws—of the wearer's body. They are comfortable and allow easy movement, but it was up to a man to make the most of his appearance, and he moved accordingly. Men doubtless found as many tricks to show off their arms and legs and figures as they were later to accuse women of adopting. For instance, a man might lightly lay a hand on hip or girdle, by the hilt of his sword, with elbow turned out; this casual posture draws the eye to the line of arm and waist and hips, with a faintly martial flavour that was doubtless very dashing. In fact this was a posture used as long as men wore swords; we find D'Artagnan in *The Three Musketeers* still affecting it. The gentlemen in Drawings 13, 47, 48, 49 and 50 are all in this position.

Fourteenth and Fifteenth Centuries. The Renaissance came late to England, but its fashions did not. For men, at least until the late fifteenth century and as far as the manner of wearing them was concerned, it was much like what we have discussed already. Of course there were variations. Long sleeves, with or without jagged edges, require care. If you aren't careful they will swing far out and hit people or catch on things. Shoes with very long pointed toes enforce a mincing step and make you careful where you put your feet. In fact, the Dandy had arrived. (One of his useful accessories was the glove; gloves, even more than shoes, can be extremely ornamental while remaining functional. If you wanted to carry them but not wear them you could, at this time, tuck them in your belt.)

The houppelande, the distinctive outer garment of the time, is the same to wear as the long tunic of earlier days, except that it has a fuller cut and more of a swing. Its long sleeve, however, was often turned back to show the lining and the tight sleeve beneath. A later fashion brought with it a new way to wear sleeves. This fashion was for a very full sleeve usually gathered at the wrist (like a modern bishop sleeve); sometimes a slit in this sleeve showed the contrasting sleeve of the garment below. When this slit was large enough you could put your arm through it and let the rest of the sleeve hang down. You can wear it or not as warmth and convenience dictate. The man and woman in Drawings 27 and 36 both have one sleeve off and one sleeve on. Pulling your sleeves on and off is a useful trick for a nervous or preoccupied man. The houppelande, long or short-skirted, was an overgarment and a cloak was rarely worn with it.

Although stylishness and finesse were beginning to come into men's manners, they still had breadth and freedom in movement. They had more freedom and lightness in clothes than before.

Another change for men was in hats, which now increased in variety. During the Middle Ages all men wore hoods. Sometimes a hat was worn as well, *over the hood*. It was fastened by a string under the chin, and when not in wear you could let it hang down your back on its string. (Chaucer so describes the Canon whose "hat hung at his bak doun by a laas.") But now there was much more choice in headgear as besides the old hoods, and hats in many new shapes, men could choose a chaperon, turban or roundlet. The last, popular in Henry IV's time and after, had a long streamer

27. Fifteenth century. He has "one sleeve off and one sleeve on."

28–31. Different ways of wearing basically similar hats.

32. The same type of hat and no fancy business.

33. Fifteenth century. An ordinary man on the way to market, not wanting to wear his hat, carries it on his shoulder in the usual way.

or liripipe which could hang straight down or be draped round the head and neck according to the wearer's fancy, and lent itself to being worn in a great variety of ways. A man could show his individuality in the way he wore his hat; Drawings 28–32 show basically similar hats worn quite differently by different men. You could lay these "hats" over one shoulder when not wearing them, which is what the man in Drawing 33, who is on his way to market, has done.

WOMEN

Thirteenth and Fourteenth Centuries. At the end of the thirteenth century women's clothes changed too. Skirts, of course, stayed long and full, but the bodice was now laced close to the figure; the loose overdress, when worn, was often cut away above to show the tight-fitting underdress, or else had loose sleeves that showed the arm in its tight sleeve beneath. You might pull your skirt through your girdle in front, to show the rich underskirt. With these long tight sleeves women, like men, began to show off their arms—so wearers of these clothes must use their arms accordingly. Remember, too, that at first it was daring to show your shape, and to hold yourself to show it off. Those who did not want to do so stayed in the old loose gowns. Fashion moved slowly then.

With the other changes came a change in headgear for women too. Hair might now sometimes be glimpsed carefully arranged in a net, or under gauze. Head tires became elaborate and often heavy—wearers must take care to balance them safely as they move or sit, yet seem to do it as a matter of course. The Wife of Bath was no more than a well-to-do middle-class woman, yet

> Hir coverchefs ful fyne weren of ground;
> I dorste swere they weyeden ten pound
> That on a Sonday weren upon hir heed.

And she doubtless wore them with a great air of nonchalance. You must look as though you wear such things without a second thought, or they lose their point. In Drawing 34 she wears a travelling hat over a smaller "coverchef" of fine

34. Fourteenth century. The Wife of Bath (Ellesmere Manuscript). She wears her broad travelling hat over her "simple" coverchef which covers every hair.

white linen. This is what she wore to ride on pilgrimage to Canterbury, so it is presumably an everyday style. Yet it is still fairly elaborate (she was a woman who enjoyed showing herself off) and it covers all her hair. Compare it with the headdress of the French miller's wife of the next century (Drawing 26) which also hides every hair. You are forced to carry your head high with such contraptions on it.

Poorer women, lower in the social scale, also let their

35. Fifteenth century. A companion of the man in Drawing 33.

fancy play a little with their headgear—after all, if you must cover your hair for decency's sake you may as well do the best you can with the covering. There was the example of the men, as well as of richer women, before you. The fourteenth-century market woman of Drawing 35 has given her hood a long tail, reminiscent of a man's liripipe. As it is inconveniently long to be left dangling behind she has pinned it up, without spoiling the effect. For women as for men there was great scope for individuality in headgear.

Fifteenth Century. By the fifteenth century ladies' dress was heavy and high waisted, with the skirt extremely full and long so that it dragged at you as you walked. Head-dresses grew larger and more elaborate, unwieldy to modern eyes though not necessarily very weighty, being often largely an arrangement of gauze on wire. You can't lean back against anything when wearing them, and must be careful going through doors. Dresses might be cut low to show off the throat, with long tight sleeves, so that all the weight came lower down.

The low neckline of this period was often low at the back as well as in front, and fashionable women would shave the hair that grew low at the back. For the neck was being seen for the first time, so it was natural to make the most of it. Remember when wearing these clothes with their tight waists, stylish sleeves and bare necks (see Drawings 36–39), that a woman was at last able to show herself off and draw attention to her physical charms in a variety of ways.

There is only one way to move in this costume which both looks and feels right. Gather up your heavy, voluminous skirt as described in Part I, and walk with head and shoulders pulled back. From the side you make a shallow C; it will help if you remember that a pregnant look was fashionable (and there were no soft chairs to sink into). Drawings 36, 37 and 38 will give you some idea of the posture, while Drawings 3, 38 and 39 show the skirt lifted.

The lady in Drawing 37 has used her leg from the knee

36. Second quarter of fifteenth century (Devonshire tapestries). The drag of her heavy dress shows in her posture; she has just let her skirt fall, and her left arm is still in position for holding it. Like the man in Drawing 27 she has "one sleeve on and one sleeve off." She is also making the most of her fashionable long neck and small waist.

37. Fifteenth century. She shows how the pull of the skirt and the
need to balance a large headdress impose the typical, correct
"C" posture.

38. Fifteenth century. A less extreme example of the same posture. Note how she holds the bulk of her skirt.

39. First half of the fifteenth century. She is using both hands to hold her skirt, and correctly holds it very high.

down to hold her skirt while she bends back slightly. This is a doubly useful trick—it keeps your skirt from getting under your feet and, together with balancing that head-dress, helps you to get the right posture. Note too that the ladies of Drawings 36 and 37, who are not holding up their skirts, have each a hand held almost horizontally in front. simply acting as an extension of the arm. Perhaps the lady in Drawing 36 has only just dropped her skirt, but the other can obviously walk quite well, though not fast, without lifting hers. For people who do not know what to do with their hands this is a quite suitable position in these clothes.

And, while in these clothes, try to avoid making a sudden turn on yourself or you will find your skirt under your feet. Walk in a curve instead and your skirt will follow you round.

40. Early sixteenth century. She is casually lifting her skirt to show the underskirt. The fall of her hood behind shows off a good carriage of the head.

Chapter 8

The Tudor Period

FROM our point of view the fashions and manners of Henry VII's reign are no more than a linking period between the quite different styles that came before and after. People wore a lot of garments at once, and the simplicity of the early Middle Ages had gone. But the general line and balance of clothes was simple, un-extreme and easy to wear.

MEN

Early Sixteenth Century. Men's legs are still much in evidence and bun-toed shoes with stiff bulbous toes are coming in. They must make it difficult to put your feet close together. In Henry VIII's time, when shoes grew larger and sleeves were padded to make you look big and broad-shouldered, fashion and convenience produced the same result. You stood with your feet apart and hands on hips or in your girdle, and looked as broad and manly as possible.

WOMEN

Early Sixteenth Century. Women's clothes were getting bulky again. Sleeves that fitted at the shoulder were very full by the time they reached the elbow, and so hands were most easily held in front, with the elbows curved out.

41. Late sixteenth century. Her hand rests on her farthingale. Note her three necklaces and the way her cap shows off her coiffure instead of hiding it.

At this time the upper skirt was often lifted, as in Drawing 40, only to show the rich petticoat below; later it was left open for the same reason. Married women began to show a little hair at the forehead, but heads were still covered.

Sixteenth Century. As the century progressed clothes grew stiffer, and less shaped to the body beneath them. By the later part of Queen Elizabeth's reign a fashionable lady's clothes were so stiff from the armpits to below the waist that her whole stance and posture were affected, becoming stiff and unnatural. This applies to both men and women of the period.

The lower classes and country people could move easily, bend freely and so on, as no fashionable person possibly could. Citizens' wives would wear a greatly modified version of the fashion. Their waists would be more natural, and they were more likely to wear decent hoods than mere bits of lace on their heads. In their clothes a woman could bustle about as was hardly possible in those grand dresses. But that was their fashionable ideal—in Beaumont and Fletcher's *Knight of the Burning Pestle* the Citizen's Wife says her tailor "had fourteen yards to make this gown." It was obviously a dress she was proud of, as fashionable as she could afford; it takes skill and practice to manage so much material with a casual air.

The correct way to manage the split skirt and the farthingale is set out in Part I; it is the same for each of the three shapes the farthingale took, which are shown in Drawings 41, 42 and 43. (The triangular shape of Drawing 42 does not seem to have been as popular as the other two in England.) Because the widest part of the farthingale is usually high up it gives the possibility of a gesture no other hooped skirt does. A famous gesture, if not ladylike; that is, Queen Elizabeth's mannish trick of slapping her thigh. In a farthingale it makes the skirt ripple; in a hoop or crinoline it would make the whole thing fly up in a manner as ludicrous as indecent. For a short time the farthingale was short enough to expose foot and ankle—a conscious exposure on the part of the wearer—but never more. This length must have given its very smart wearer a sense of daring too; but she still kept her steps small.

42. c. 1585. Note the arms held away from the body—this shows off her waist and is probably necessary in these extremely stiff clothes.

In stiff Elizabethan clothes it was easier to keep one's arm movements high—anyone who knows how even a modern, lightly boned, foundation garment can chafe will know why. In the sixteenth century corsets were made of wood, whalebone, even steel. Drawing 44 shows one, now in the Wallace Collection, which is made of steel;

43. c. 1590. Again her hands rest on the swell of her skirt. Note the jewel on her sleeve.

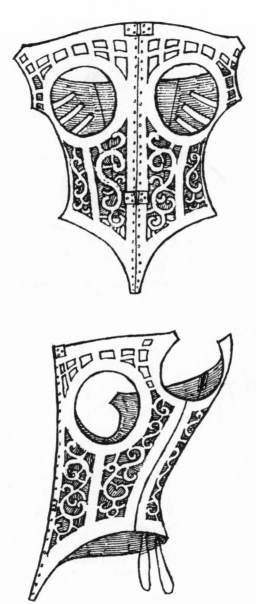

44. Sixteenth century. Steel corsets, the frame-
work filled in with steel openwork. They were
originally lined and covered.

it was originally lined and covered. Wearing such a garment you can't easily twist or bend, and you will find it easier to turn right round than to make a half turn without moving your feet. As for bending, it is unlikely you would want to, even assuming you could do so with ease; for the décolleté of these styles was so extremely low as to be often indecent to our eyes. (A low neckline was officially for unmarried girls, while anyone could wear her dress close to the throat.)

The fashionable corset pushed the breasts as high as possible, forcing the shoulders back. At the same time a high collar or close ruff forced you to hold your head poised high and carefully. Altogether, the only possible posture was stiff and unnatural; yet it was necessary to appear relaxed and at ease. This was probably easier than we think, since it would not have occurred to the women of the time to think their own clothes awkward or to consider dressing differently. One's own fashions always seem so obviously *right* that a more comfortable dress would have looked dowdy or eccentric to them.

In repose the hands must lie on the swell of the farthingale, but there are different ways of doing this. You can hold both hands level, or at different heights, they can both lie on the "shelf" of your farthingale or both at its edge as in Drawing 6, or one hand can droop over the edge as in Drawings 45 and 46. Arms were usually held away from the body, with the elbow bent out to emphasize a narrow waist; but occasionally a woman might hold them parallel with her body, the lower arm turning out across the wheel of her farthingale in an oddly sophisticated attitude that emphasized the unnaturalness of the fashionable shape.

At this time some women openly used cosmetics. It was by no means a universal practice as it is today, but it was an accepted one. Moralists violently disapproved of it, and they were right for prosaic reasons apart from their principles. For the materials used were dangerous; they

45. Very early seventeenth century (fashions were still unchanged).
Her arms are held away from her body; one hand on the widest
part of her farthingale, and the other drooping over it.

included red and white lead, and blindness was the occupational disease of the workmen who made some of them. The long-term effect of regularly using these concoctions must have been as foul as anything a preacher could have invented. But the attitude to life, and the behaviour, of people who openly wear make-up is different from that of those who don't think of doing so.

By the end of the century great ladies were going about bare-headed, although they usually wore at least a token piece of lace or an ornament in their hair. In 1575 a Dutch visitor noticed that English women often went out of doors without hood or mantle; but that married women, on the other hand, wore hats indoors as well as out. In those days the details of fashion (and, therefore, the behaviour clothes imposed on their wearers) varied from country to country.

Gloves, of course, were much worn and could indeed be used to show how distant (or not) you wanted to keep an admirer. If a gentleman went to kiss a lady's gloved hand it was a mark of particular favour if she took her glove off for him.

A lady could wear jewels almost anywhere. This was an age when people dressed as richly and ostentatiously as they could. There was not much point in wearing bracelets with those long, elaborate sleeves, but three necklaces at once (as in Drawing 41) were quite allowable. Earrings were popular too, now that the ears were at last uncovered. Jewels could be pinned to one's sleeve (as in Drawing 43) and worn in the hair (as in Drawing 46), and sometimes they were even pinned on the ruff. There was no restraint about it, you could wear jewels in all these places at once, as well as rings on your fingers and jewelled buttons to ornament your dress—if you were rich enough.

It was at the end of this period that the folding fan first appeared, although it was not widely used for another century. (Queen Catherine de' Medici introduced it to

46. Very early seventeenth century (sixteenth century fashions still unchanged). One hand rests on the shelf of her farthingale, the other is over the edge. Note the jewels and ornament in her hair.

France and the fashion spread.) The stiff fan (see Drawings 42 and 46) in its different forms was much more common. But the management of the fan was not brought to such polished perfection at this time as it was later.

MEN

Sixteenth Century. Men's clothes (at least those of the fashionable upper classes) grew like the women's—stiff and unyielding with high close ruffs and aiming at small waists—with the same effect of unbending stiffness in their posture and movements, with arms held slightly away from the body, etc. They carried a great deal of padding, too, both in the sleeves and on the hips. You virtually upholstered any chair you sat on! Men were trying to show their virility, wearing codpieces (a small stuffed bag placed at the fork of the legs, which was first worn in the preceding century) and with their legs on show again. Beatrice in *Much Ado About Nothing* lists "a good leg and a good foot" as desirable attributes for a man. And the elaborate ruffs they wore at their wrists were doubtless meant to draw the eye, which implies a conscious use of the hands, at least by the dandy. After all, a man could always wear a plain starched cuff if he chose. The Osric type of accomplished courtier kissed his hand as he bowed— a way to show off hands and legs at once besides being, doubtless, the height of affectation.

The easiest way to hold your arms in these clothes is to let one hand lie lightly on the hilt of your sword or beside it, while the other rests on your hip or your padded trunk hose (see Drawings 13, 47 and 48). There are many variations of this, partly depending on the precise shape of your trunk hose—such details of fashion changed frequently. Although the easiest posture, and therefore most typical, it was not, of course, the only one.

Jewels were as popular with men as with women. The

47. c. 1560. He typically has his arms akimbo, with one hand lying by his sword-hilt. Besides his two chains and the jewel that clasps the feather in his hat, his clothes are covered with jewelled buttons.

gentleman of Drawing 47, who has dressed finely to have his picture painted, shows the contemporary attitude. There are at least eighty jewelled buttons on his clothes in the original; the expensive curled feather in his hat is held by a large jewelled clasp; and he is wearing two necklaces. At this time men wore earrings too, although he is not doing so. One manner of wearing a pendant jewel, to be seen in many pictures of men of this period, is to hang it on a broad, soft ribbon tied at the back of the neck. The jewel in these pictures is large and circular, such as the gentleman in Drawing 47 wears on a chain, and may well be a miniature in a jewelled case.

There was a variety of styles of short cloak for men to choose from, or change to with the fashion, as well as the great cloak for travelling or bad weather. But they must still be worn pulled up on to one shoulder, if not both (see Drawings 13, 14 and 48). There was nothing impolite in a man's wearing his hat indoors at this date.

The famous English habit of this time, of kissing freely on coming and going, has been too widely commented on to need more than a passing reference here. It seems to have applied to all classes.

This was, I think, the latest period when the pomander was commonly used by either sex. On the other hand the handkerchief was coming into more general use, so those who like to have something to clutch have a wider choice from this time on. A short list of the obvious things at this time includes handkerchiefs, gloves, fans (both kinds), sword hilts, jewels (you might perhaps finger the chain you wear) or even your clothes, though this should only be a last resort.

It was in the late sixteenth century that shoes with heels were first worn. They must have caused many stiff legs and sprained ankles at first, and doubtless the older generation did not take to them at all. It seems to have been a

48. 1568. He holds his arms in the same way as the gentleman in Drawing 47. Note the cloak over one shoulder.

fashion that spread fast, once it came in. Out of doors a pantofle was often worn over the shoe. It was rather like a large heel-less mule and must have made its wearers shuffle to some extent. It would be worn instead of the patten.

49. 1639. The stiffness has gone from clothes and posture. Note the hand by the sword-hilt.

Chapter 9

The Seventeenth
and Eighteenth Centuries

First Half of Seventeenth Century. There was no abrupt change at the turn of the century. For a while men's clothes were bulkily padded in imitation of King James. This must of course have made their movements clumsier; but it also meant less rigidity of clothes and therefore less angular attitudes. Later there was a general softening of the outline, farthingales and stiffness went quite out of fashion and soft, willowy movements were possible. Drawing 49 shows an intermediate stage in men's clothes; there is no stiffness though plenty of bulk, soft lace at neck and wrist and rather a lot of shirt sleeve shown at the wrist, yet a large slash (to show the shirt) in each sleeve. His posture is much the same as his father's, but he no longer needs to hold his body so rigid.

For the first time the lower part of women's arms was bared—they doubtless were very conscious of this "advance" and displayed their arms accordingly. This was also a time when dresses were lower-cut than at any other; we should think their necklines indecent, but a fashionable lady of the time would be quite unconcerned. Puritanical or middle-class women (often the same), of course, felt and behaved differently.

50. Mid-seventeenth century. The dandy (still with hand on hip) wears boots that force him to stride and swagger.

51. 1654. Her skirt is loosely twisted and lifted at the side, out of the dirt. Sleeves are shorter than ever before, enabling her to show off her arms.

Everyone had heels to his or her shoes now. When it was fashionable for men to wear boots, especially those with "Cavalier" bucket tops, a certain swagger inevitably came into their walk. You can't walk in those boots without one, as Drawing 50 shows, for the gentleman can't bring his feet together without crushing both his boot tops and their lace-edged lining. In any case, a man who dresses like this is plainly showing off his finery. His staff seems to be more a fashionable accessory than any actual help to him.

The "Cavalier and Roundhead" difference in costume depended entirely on simplicity and colour. For women there was also the difference of neckline, and the fact that a "Puritan" woman had a simpler and more complete head covering. Any difference in movement and manner— and this could be considerable—arose from character, personality, personal ideas of propriety, and circumstance, not from anything else. The basic rule still holds good. Hold yourself well, allow for the sweep of your sword and the folds of your cloak if a man, and know how to move in your skirt if a woman.

Skirts were no longer open in front. To keep your skirt clean when out in foul, muddy weather you must pull it tight round the knees then, with all the fullness gathered in front, lift it as in Drawing 51. Lowered later, it will hide any splashes on your petticoat, which was not lifted. It is worth commenting on the fact that this young lady has covered her head to go out, even though the transparent stuff is more of a token than anything else. Still, it will keep her hair tidy and protect her face a little from the weather—a white, smooth skin was considered a mark of beauty. And nobody can accuse her of going out bareheaded.

MEN

Restoration. Reaction came with the Restoration. Women's clothes were little altered, except in detail, but the men

52. c. 1678. Note how he turns out his toes and rests his weight on his staff (worn with sword).

really went to town. Their clothes grew extremely elaborate, with bunches of ribbon and petticoat breeches, etc., like the gentleman in Drawing 50. A great deal of shirt showed too; the general effect of a smart man's appearance was that at any moment his outer clothes would fall off and he be left standing in his shirt. Very sexy, at the time. In these clothes they were more or less bound to hold their legs apart and their arms away from the body. So they swaggered around and wore their clothes with an air. Friends were still likely to kiss on meeting, but this was beginning to seem affected.

The business men—merchants, lawyers, etc.—dressed and behaved more simply to match the different lives they led. But a young fellow setting out to be very smart would try to copy the aristocracy in clothes and manner. As a man's attitude to life shows in his manners, so his manner will show how used he is to the clothes he wears.

In 1666 Charles II changed the whole style of the fashionable man's wardrobe; they took to the ensemble of coat, waistcoat, knee breeches and stockings that they wore, with variations, to the end of the eighteenth century. Drawing 52 is a typical man of the period. He has apparently paused to speak to a friend and is leaning on his staff while the other hand lies on his hip. On his head he balances a large hat and wig (unless that superb head of hair could be his own) and his feet are in a position we would connect with fashion models and ballet dancers.

In these clothes the shape of a man's legs showed. That they were very conscious of their legs is proved by the cartoons of men with padded calves, and by such literary and theatrical comment as Lord Foppington's concern about the thickness of his stockings (in *The Relapse*, 1696). That they had reason to think seriously about the matter is demonstrated by Queen Caroline herself. Lord Hervey in his Memoirs quotes a conversation he held with her in 1735 about Sir Robert Walpole, when she named Sir

53. A French prince. His feet are almost in the fourth ballet position. Note how he carries his hat tucked under his arm and holds his glove in the same hand, leaving the other free.

Robert's swollen legs and ugly paunch as equal objects of
aversion to any woman who might otherwise be attracted
by him.

These were the days when ballet was developing and,
as stated in Part I, it was largely based on contemporary
style. So it is worth while to consider the positions of the
feet in classical ballet when you are thinking how a man of
the late seventeenth and eighteenth centuries placed his.
Ballet, using highly trained people, has gone to extremes
but the relationship is still very close. You can see it in
Drawings 52–55, and the relationship is in more than the
feet.

Fops of the sixteen-nineties had, for a time, a fashion of
holding their heads tilted to one side. As they loved to lay
down the law about everything they probably thought it
gave them a judicious air.

Late Seventeenth and Eighteenth Centuries. A certain stiff
uprightness came back into the gentleman's posture, and
elderly dandies took to wearing corsets. All gentlemen of
this period learned to dance and fence, which was bound to
affect the placing of their feet and the carriage of their
bodies; an obvious though subtle class distinction, giving
them an air not to be gained by parvenus. It partly
explains, perhaps, the apparent relationship with ballet
mentioned above. The gentleman in Drawing 56 is dressed—
and stands—to show off his figure. Yet he somehow lacks
the high polish of the highest class; perhaps he belongs to
the lesser gentry, or is trying to raise himself into their
ranks. It is a subtle distinction worth noting. An actor who
can use his technique to get it across will have gone a
great way towards placing his character.

Since coats were often made of beautiful materials that
should not be crushed, a man on sitting down would automatically draw the skirts of his coat from under him.
(By now a man's class could usually be told by more than
the materials his clothes were made of; usually the clothes

54. Eighteenth century. Even sitting down he holds his arms and legs as stylishly as he can.

55. Eighteenth century. A very polite gentleman. Note the position of his legs and feet.

of the lower classes were simpler, as well as easier to wear.) Any man who had been to a good school, and every well-trained servant, had learnt to hold himself well.

Another point for the actor to note is that a servant in close attendance on his master for any length of time would probably pick up some of his mannerisms, if he did not try to copy his whole manner. This would be partly unconscious of course, but partly deliberate, to impress his friends and fellows with the superiority he "shared" with his master.

The precise hand movements of the eighteenth-century gentleman, which actors make great play with, were partly forced on him by his clothes. When you wear expensive lace ruffles you will naturally shake them out of the way before doing anything, rather than risk damaging them. Thus even the most affected, dandiacal movements have some functional basis. Then this was the age of snuff-taking, and snuff gets all over the place. All but the most expert users need to brush themselves down after taking it. The scope this gives to a dandy or Macaroni is obvious, especially if added to a wish to show off his snuffbox and his fine lace.

During most of this period gentlemen often carried a long stick when walking. (This remained usual until after the 1914–1918 war.) For your dandy the "nice conduct of a clouded cane," as Pope put it, was an important matter; but it was more than a dandy's adjunct, especially when wearing swords went out of fashion. Obviously, you might use your stick while walking, and lean on it with one or both hands when sitting still. Or you might rest it on the ground behind you, clasped in one or both hands, and lean back on it. Or hold it with both hands horizontally behind you. (The gentleman in Drawing 57 is leaning on it while he crosses his legs in a relaxed pose that—again—unconsciously makes the most of the shape of his legs.) There are of course other positions for it, but these are the most comfortable and usual.

56. 1745. A smart gentleman who somehow lacks style. Compare him with the preceding four figures.

There are several correct and "typical" postures for a man among friends and acquaintances. He can push his coat back to put one hand on his hip beneath it; or raise a side-flap, if his coat has one, to put his hand behind it and into his breeches' pocket; or he can thrust one hand into his open upper waistcoat. He carries his hat in the crook of his arm (as in Drawing 53) or under his arm. If, as sometimes happened, he wore a muff, it was slung at his waist in front.

Your precise posture and poise, of course, varies with the person; from the graceless swagger of the Mohocks (those upper-crust young men who terrorized the streets of London) to the mincing gait of the high-heeled Macaronis. These last flourished in the seventeen-seventies and wore their wigs so high that they sometimes affected using a cane to lift their hats!

The wigs worn throughout this period imposed a certain control and balance on one's walk. The large, full-bottomed ones gave an air of stateliness to their wearer. The lighter, smaller wigs that came later must have been easy to knock sideways or back—every man who cared about his appearance must have glanced into any mirror he passed for a quick check.

That eighteenth-century men found wig-wearing tiresome (though they would not admit it publicly by word or sign) is shown by the fact that they unwigged themselves in private. A gentleman *en négligé* removed his wig and covered his cropped head with a cap or turban; he took off his fine coat and put on a full-length dressing gown—also well cut and of fine material if he could afford it, but of tougher stuff. This was a much more comfortable outfit and most gentlemen wore it at home, changing into wig and coat before going out or receiving company. Some, casual or ill-mannered, did not always bother, occasioning the third of the rules laid down by Beau Nash in 1707 for the Bath society he governed: "That Gentlemen of Fashion never

57. Eighteenth century. A quietly dressed gentleman relaxes, leaning on his cane.

appearing in a Morning before the Ladies in Gowns and Caps show Breeding and Respect." Note that even ill-bred boors did not *dream* of appearing in their shirts.

WOMEN

Late Seventeenth Century. Women's clothes changed much more during this period. They soon had a great variety of outdoor things to put on—shawl, tippet, hood, muff, scarf, gloves, mask, etc. When Lady Fanciful (*The Provoked Wife*, 1697) prepared to go out to a rendez-vous she wrapped herself up in a shawl, hat and mask, and gloves of course. The great cloak was now little used by the upper classes, except for travelling. Make-up was used again by some women. Ladies in Restoration plays often refer to it when being catty, and Lady Wishfort, the mutton-dressed-up-as-lamb (*The Way of the World*, 1700) is first seen in her dressing room ordering her maid to "fetch me a little red . . . the Spanish paper, idiot, complexion . . . Paint."

At first clothes kept their simple, flowing, unconstricting shape (see Drawings 7 and 58). Then bodices stiffened, and once the stiff-boned bodice had come into fashion it stayed for over a hundred years. Women's backs, and their general carriage, grew correspondingly stiffer. Sometimes the stiff bodices, shaped rather like corsets, ended *under* the breasts, which were covered by a fichu (there were at least four different ways to wear the fichu). In novels gay gentlemen frequently disarrange the chambermaid's kerchief (another name for the fichu)—a pastime more exciting for the man and embarrassing to the girl than it seems to modern readers. On the other hand a stiff, tight bodice that came high enough for decency left a sort of pocket between the breasts; the woman hiding compromising letters and other articles in the bosom of her dress really did have somewhere to put them.

Arms follow the long line of the bodice. Instead of clasping

your hands try a fashionable variant of the time; cross them
just above the wrist, with one hand laid on the opposite
lower arm and held below the waist (see Drawing 59 and

58. c. 1660. Clothes are more comfortable than they have been
for a long time. Note that she sits with her knees apart.

60). When small waists are fashionable it is often a good
idea to emphasize one by curving your elbows out, so that
it is framed in a noticeable blank space. Conversely, you
might hide or lessen the apparent thickness of a waist by
skilful placing of the arms; but only a woman who spends
much care and trouble on her appearance would bother

59. 1688. Note how her arms follow the line of the bodice, with one hand clasping the other arm above the wrist.

60. 1689. Like the lady of Drawing 59 she holds her arms to emphasize the fashionable line. Note how her high fontange and flowing lappets emphasize the carriage of her head.

to do that. To be successful at it you need to practise in front of a mirror, a full-length one if possible.

The next fashion in skirts was to lift the overskirt high in front, looping it back over the hips and later tying it right back (see Drawings 59, 60 and 61). A pretty fashion, but one with problems for walking in. Strictly speaking, you can't lift the overskirt. However, to keep it out of the mud you may sometimes twist it up and bring it round to one side, where you will hold it at about knee level (see Drawing 61). This is awkward and does not look well, so it should be dropped as soon as possible. The other problem is to prevent the overskirt dragging back when you turn. You can't use your hands. Instead, bring your hips round on the turn with a sharp, clean movement and the skirt will come with them. To get the precise movement requires practice; once you have got it you will find it invaluable in wearing this dress, giving you style and elegance as well as freedom.

About 1688 women's hair began to be dressed high, and their head-dresses rose too, in a tower of lace called a fontange. You must hold your head to balance it—and remember to allow for its height when entering doors. The fontange usually had long lace lappets (see Drawings 59, 60 and 61). These usually hang behind, where their straight line emphasizes a good carriage of the head. To keep them out of the way they were sometimes loosely knotted above the breast. The lady in Drawing 61 has her overskirt held up and the lappets of her headdress knotted; she is obviously going out of doors.

Seventeenth and Eighteenth Centuries. When using your arms in these clothes remember that, in the stiff bodices, it is most comfortable to hold your arms up, away from your body. Consider the upper arms of the lady in Drawing 62, for instance, as she holds her hat in one hand and lets the other rest on the swell of her skirt. As with men, it is useful to consider the ballet, particularly the basic *port de bras*,

61. 1687. The overskirt loosely twisted up and lifted out of the dirt. Note the lappets of her cap are knotted loosely so as not to damage the lace.

for the relationship, although distant, is a helpful guide to getting the right sort of style for these clothes.

Fans. These were now in regular use (the folding fan, that is, which had superseded the old rigid kind) and you can do a lot with them. Hold them, open or shut; signal with them; count the sticks coyly; "peep in them" to hide your face, for embarrassment or some other reason; even break them in a temper. But remember that you must use your whole arm when wielding a fan. Movement from the wrist only is too small, jerky and stiff; let it flow from the shoulder.

It is best to close your fan when not using it, but this is not absolutely necessary. Drawings 63 and 64 show how you can let your hand lie upon the swell of your hoop while holding an open fan. This, although not very graceful, gives an actress increased scope in using a fan for emphasis, since gently lowering it and later closing it can be made into two separate gestures.

In the large hoop of the mid-eighteenth century you must remember that you take up a lot of space, and that the hoop itself is inclined to bounce about. You can read how to walk in a hoop in Part I. Notice the left hand of the lady in Drawing 63, which is empty and apparently rests idly on the swell of her hoop. She has placed it as far as she can comfortably reach, and is using it to keep her hoop still and to guide it as she walks. An extremely wide hoop might force you to go through doors sideways.

Men must not press too near a lady in a hoop, for obvious reasons. This had its points; Anna Howe, the friend and correspondent of Clarissa Harlowe, commented that a hoop was useful for keeping men at a distance. In any case, it was dangerously easy for a hoop to show too much. As one wit said when they were at their largest:

> A hoop eight yards wide
> May decently show your garters are tied.

62. c. 1740. Note how she holds her upper arms away from her body, and the free hand rests on the swell of her skirt.

Drawing 65, which is taken from a 1745 cartoon, shows how ugly, as well as improper, a badly managed hoop could be. The lady is showing a great deal of leg as well as the bottom

63. 1777 Court costume. Note how her hands lie on the swell of her skirt.

of her chemise (she will be wearing her petticoat between her hoop and her dress, so that no ridges show). She would find a sudden gust of wind, or a slight trip, extremely disconcerting to say the least.

However, the hoop itself had some flexibility, and you could crush it into a slightly narrower shape with your hands. In the seventeen-forties, when skirts were narrow

64. Eighteenth century. A possible way to hold a fan.

"fore and aft" but wide at the sides, you could genteelly lift your hoop at one side. Or, when walking, a discreet tilt could show your ankles and pretty petticoat for a moment.

65. 1745. From a Boitard cartoon—how *not* to handle a hoop.

One way and another, a lady's modesty was precarious for much of this century.

The Watteau-like dress, or sacque, which had pleats falling straight down the back from neck to hem over a hoop, remained as part of court dress long after it went out of fashion in the first quarter of the eighteenth century. And if you fail to stand perfectly when wearing it—everybody knows! But at this date little girls were put into corsets, so to stand straight was second nature by the time you were adult, and any other posture would be uncomfortable. Then, although the bodice was stiff and constricting, the hoop was the opposite. No one had to worry about keeping her stomach firm and flat as we do today.

The elaborate high powdered headdress worn for part of this period (roughly 1760–80) must have caused many a stiff neck and aching head. Any violent movement would bring down a shower of powder, if no more. But whether their hair was elaborately or simply dressed most women wore something on their heads, usually a cap like the ladies in Drawings 62 and 64; at the least an ornament. The lady in Drawing 63 is wearing a fanciful headdress with her court dress. Even with the flat straw hat that was fashionable for a time the cap was kept on underneath; in the cartoon (Drawing 65) the frill of a cap shows underneath the hat, and the lady of Drawing 62 has been wearing her hat over her cap.

Chapter 10

Late Eighteenth and
Early Nineteenth Centuries

WOMEN

By the seventeen-nineties the hoop was quite out of fashion. Padding round the hips, under extremely full skirts, emphasized a women's shape for a time. Curves were the thing, and the natural shape. A comparison of Drawing 66 with Drawings 62, 63, 64 and 65 shows how complete the change was. In the Empire fashion that quickly followed you could see a woman's own shape for the very first time (even corsets were sometimes left off)—even the shape of the legs could be seen! The whole arm was bare for the first time too. Remember that, to the women wearing these clothes and the men seeing them, this was an entirely new fashion, a really exciting one.

English fashions were never so extreme as in France, although our high-waisted dresses were flimsy enough, worn with few underclothes, and did little to disguise the figure. At the very end of the century stays were barely six inches long, and for a time the most fashionable women wore none. At this time, when dresses were flimsy and often transparent, some women (the fast ones who wore these clothes) wore pantaloons for decency. Those who needed to wear

66. 1798. A softer stance and carriage of the arm go with the new fashion—willowy and following the line of the body.

67. 1802. The arms follow the straight line of fashion; note how she holds her skirt.

68. 1802. She holds her arms so as not to break the line of her skirt (compare the crossed arms of the ladies in Drawings 59 and 60). Note that she wears a cap.

them doubtless allowed themselves nearly as great freedom of movement as of dress.

The extreme fashion did not last long, and early in the new century skirts were cut very full and worn with plenty of petticoats. These all blew out alarmingly in the wind, and gave rise to a lot of new cartoons, and doubtless gave their wearers a lot of new preoccupations, too. It was, however, no wonder that the style stayed popular for twenty years despite the cartoonists. For it was less restrictive and allowed greater freedom of movement in every way than had been possible for generations. The line was long, straight and high-waisted, and obviously you held yourself and your arms to follow the general line.

This meant, usually, a straight line from the shoulder, but soft and willowy, not rigid; as in Drawings 66 and 67. If you did want to fold your arms—though this is ungraceful—then you followed the waistline as in Drawing 68. Compare this with Drawings 59 and 60 and you will see in what different ways you can cross your arms. Although Drawing 69 comes from a picture of 1823 the basic fashion is still unchanged. Her dress allows the movement of her legs to be seen even at Almack's, the height of respectability; notice that, as she moves in the dance, one arm is stretched out freely from the shoulder while the other follows the line of her dress.

For all the new freedom, children were still trained with backboards, and deportment in general was unimpaired.

Caps were still worn, although a girl at a grand ball might put feathers or other ornaments in her hair instead. Jane Austen's letters, even more than her novels, demonstrate the necessity and importance of caps to the ordinary woman. If you couldn't afford a new dress you might manage a new cap, perhaps by taking an old one to pieces and re-making it. You were always on the look-out for a new and becoming style, and exchanging cap patterns was a sign of friendship. Harriette Wilson, the famous courtesan of

69. 1823 (at Almacks). Note the line of her free movements.

Regency days, showed her independence of convention by wearing her hair loose, without any covering or ornament. She did this to show off her hair, which was apparently one of her great charms; but she makes such a point of it in her memoirs that it was obviously an unusual, daring thing worth drawing the reader's attention to.

Stoles were much worn at this time. They later developed into the popular shawl, and there was much similarity in draping them. There is quite an art in this, one well worth studying, as skilful use of a stole enables you to hide the bad points of your figure and to show off the good ones. This is something each woman must work out for herself, since each person is different, but here as a basis to work from is a short list of positions for a stole or shawl (some can be seen in Drawings 82, 83 and 84): around the neck, with both ends hanging level; resting in the crook of the arms, and looped across the back; the same thing but held between shoulder and elbow; around both shoulders; on one shoulder and off the other; just off both shoulders; high on one arm and low on the other.

Reticules were now carried because there was nowhere to put the traditional pocket. A small price to pay for the comfort of the costume; you could relax in it in a way that had never been possible before.

MEN

Men were less fortunate. Their fashions changed too, but less completely. Wigs went out of fashion and they wore their own hair short, and often deliberately disordered. This did not take all constriction from the carriage of the head, however, for coat collars now rose up to the ears behind. This draws attention to a good carriage, but you must be careful to avoid chafing. Don't hope to take the easy if ugly way out by poking your head forward. You won't be able to do it, for the high and elaborately folded

70. 1805. Note how pantaloons and boots show off his legs; his toes turned out; his high shirt collar and coat collar; the hat and cane in his hand; and his fob.

cravat came into fashion at the same time. You must hold your head at a very precise angle or ruin your clothes.

As a matter of visual balance elaborate wrist ruffles shrank out of fashion, and so the careful hand movements of the preceding century faded out too.

The wish to show off their limbs affected men as much as women, and they took to wearing skin-tight pantaloons (see Drawing 70). These made a well-turned leg an important part of a man's appearance—the whole leg, not just from the knee down. It was about this time that braces were invented. They were useful to the man wearing these tight pantaloons, and doubtless made a subtle difference to the bearing of their wearers. Modern men can work this out in practice with belts and braces.

The tight pantaloon was soon accompanied by tight coats, also cut to show the shape beneath (helped on occasion by both padding and corsets). In these a fine pair of shoulders and arms could show to as much advantage as good legs in the pantaloons below. Beau Brummell's ideal of understated elegance depended on the cut of your clothes and the casual way you wore them. Either could easily be carried to a new extreme. In any case, a man who had spent hours knotting his high cravat into perfect shape would be likely to carry himself to show off his work. In practice this means sticking your chest out. The cravat was soon reinforced by high shirt collars, with points rising to the cheeks. (See Drawings 71–74.) The dandy's ensemble must have been more uncomfortable about the neck than the Elizabethan's with his wide, starched ruff.

The gentleman of this time usually wore a fob ornament which could be very ornamental indeed, and might be a useful object for a nervous man to play with. The gentleman in Drawing 70 carries a hat and stick as well. Small hands and feet were considered as great beauties in a man as in a woman; so those who had them showed them off.

71. About 1820. "Going to White's" (Lord Alvanley) by
R. Dighton. Note the extremely high shirt collar and how large
he looks above the waist, controlled below—top-heavy to our
eyes. His head is almost extinguished.

72. About 1820. The Marquis of Worcester by R. Dighton.
Naturally slimmer than Lord Alvanley, he displays the same
top-heaviness and care to mark his waist.

73. About 1820. "A Big-Wig" (Mr. Wombwell) by R. Dighton.
This gentleman, aiming at the same top-heavy effect, is plainly
wearing corsets. Note how he holds his hat.

Chapter 11

The Nineteenth Century and Since

THE fashion that came in at the end of the eighteenth century remained for some time, modified rather than altered. The cloak had now quite gone out of fashion, though women partly revived it later with the cape. Now they wore pelisses (a garment rather like a modern coat). Men took to the long, caped overcoat, a garment that can be worn with great style.

MEN

Early Nineteenth Century. Men continued to show off their figures and push out their chests in close fitting clothes. This meant that a number of them wore stays, especially elderly men who fancied themselves (the Prince Regent is a famous example) although a portly—not fat!—figure was fashionable. The full coat skirts of the previous century were cut back into swallow-tails; be careful when you sit down to flick them casually out of the way.

Contemporary cartoons, concerned with lampooning individuals rather than mocking fashion, provide Drawings 71-76; their subjects (all but one) are either very fashionable or trying to be so. The men of Drawings 71 and 72

74. 1822. By R. Dighton. A would-be smart young man about town. Note the emphasized waist and the cane tucked under his arm.

are portly, puffing out their chests and proud of it. Drawing 73 is puffing out his chest too, but appears to be firmly corseted below; in fact, Drawing 72 may be corseted too, but more discreetly. The youths of Drawings 74 and 75, who are less able to take fashion in their stride (extremes always look silly), are showing off small waists below their puffed-out chests.

All of them have quite startlingly high collars that are liable to cut their ears and bury their chins. This was another fashion that lasted a very long time, and although details of the collars and cravats altered their effect on the wearer was still the same. The middle-class man of Drawing 76 who is less fashionable than the others (I should say more conservative as he is clinging to an older fashion) has his head wedged as uncomfortably high as the others. Plain starched shirt cuffs that showed at the wrist complemented these high collars.

Regency bucks took a great interest in boxing, often becoming quite competent boxers themselves. So there was a set deliberately copying the uncouth demeanour of the prize fighter as a form of showing off. You can use this to bring variety into the setting of a Regency play—but remember that the most extreme followers of the Fancy would revert to normal good manners before ladies.

As time went on the tight coat and pantaloons changed their shape. Sleeves were for a while puffed at the shoulder, and peg-top trousers came in (see Drawing 77). None of this made much difference to posture or movement. Waists are still important. The long staff of a century ago nearly vanished and the shorter cane came into fashion. This could be carried with the hat (as in Drawings 70 and 80) or tucked under the arm (as in Drawings 74 and 77). High hats were coming into fashion. Although they differed in detail from a modern topper, practice with an ordinary top hat will enable you to carry one off. Worn at an angle, they could give a jaunty air. A tap on the crown,

75. 1823. By R. Dighton. This vulgar young man has not missed
any feature of the dress of the preceding elegant gentlemen; he
has the small tight waist, is as stout as can be above it and has a
very high shirt collar.

after setting it in place, ensured its fitting snugly. Note that this hat, when carried, is usually held by the edge of the brim. The exception shown here (Drawing 80) is from a Punch cartoon showing Sir Robert Peel standing beside

76. Early eighteen-twenties. "At Lloyds" by R. Dighton. An older man in an older fashion, he is still forced to hold his head carefully.

Queen Victoria's chair; there is always an extra deference in behaviour when in the presence of royalty.

Gloves were an indispensable part of a gentleman's attire, no longer merely functional or ornamental articles. They were worn much more than today; for instance at balls, now that people touched each other so much when dancing, gloves were worn all the evening.

At this time the whole art of tailoring changed, and men's clothes were cut with the same techniques as are

77. 1829. The shape of his legs no longer shows; but his waist does. Note his cane.

used today. In fact there has been no change in men's clothes since, except in details. You sometimes hear it said that, before this time, men's clothes were very badly cut. This is only true if you judge by today's standards, but we are aiming at something different. An eighteenth-century coat of fine brocade was cut to show off the material, being comfortable enough for its wearer who was showing himself off too. He would probably consider today's clothes badly cut by his standards. But from this time the point of a man's clothes was not (at least overtly) to show off the man. The cut of a coat was in itself of the greatest importance, the aim being to make it fit as well as one's skin while allowing perfect freedom of movement. So a modern man will feel more immediately at home in these clothes than in those of earlier times, though earlier styles can be very comfortable.

By the eighteen-thirties men's trouser legs are loose and they are no longer showing off the shape of their legs. Mrs. Grundy is appearing on the scene, and her effect on everyone's behaviour does not need expatiating on. Flamboyance faded out, for one thing, and arm and hand movements became small and unobtrusive. A brief exception to this rule were the dandies who, led by Count D'Orsay, flourished in the 'thirties. They tended to wear their coats almost sliding off their shoulders, exposing a splendid expanse of chest (see Drawing 78). At least that was the idea, but the result depended on a man's physique. D'Orsay himself was a fine figure of a man, but these dandies were quite content to use stays and padding.

Cravats had shrunk, and at this time the showiest part of a gentleman's costume was his starched and frilled shirt front. It really was important—how many times do you come across silly girls (in novels by Dickens and others, and no doubt it happened in real life too) claiming that they had fallen in love with a gentlemen's linen?

Shirt cuffs continued to be starched too, and the practice

78. 1834. Count d'Orsay. The ideal of many.

of shooting cuffs had arrived—that is, pulling them down below the coat sleeve to make sure enough starched linen showed. Men don't seem to shoot their cuffs now but it was a common habit, sometimes developing into a nervous trick, of the men of the nineteenth and early twentieth centuries.

Another habit which has fallen into disuse is the graduated handshake. Most useful in a snobbish society, it was a method of putting people in their place, or else pleasing them with your affability, without being at all rude. Today we either shake hands or we don't. There used to be more choice—you could offer one, two or three fingers instead of the whole hand. You will find frequent references to it in the novelists of the time. The graduated handshake was not confined to men, of course. Becky Sharp (of *Vanity Fair*) for instance was delighted to put George Osborne in his place, as soon as she was in a position to do so, by simply offering him her right forefinger to shake, just as he thought he would show magnanimity by (not very kindly) offering her his whole hand, but the left one.

Mid-century. In the middle of the nineteenth century, when social etiquette was elaborate, you could usually tell a man's class from his appearance. Fashions worked their way down the social ladder. When the gentleman was rather drearily dressed and carefully measuring the amount of shirt front he showed (more of it at night or in summer), the flamboyance of earlier generations would still appear in the bourgeoisie. You can see the sort of thing in the vulgar showiness of Surtees' Mr. Jorrocks, and such gentlemen. Their manner varied too. While the "true" gentleman was unostentatiously showing off his gleaming shirt front and the cut of his waistcoat, Mr. Jorrocks was laying himself out to show off a glory of bright colours and cheap jewellery. (The jewellery a man could decently wear was rings, watch and chain, shirt studs, and a stick-pin in his cravat.) In the same way some of Dickens' minor characters glory in high

79. 1846. The collar is not so high now, but the small waist is still there. Note how he carries hat and cane in one hand.

points to their shirt collars long after these had gone out of fashion.

Drawing 79 is an ideal back view of a gentleman in the eighteen-forties, still aiming at a small waist, while Drawing 80 is the real thing holding his hat, cane and gloves as he stands respectfully before the Queen. The old gracefulness had gone. Gentlemen no longer automatically learnt to fence, although little boys were still sent to dancing classes. Instead, stays were still frequently worn. The average Englishman's gait looked stiff and awkward, without elasticity, to the eye of a foreigner; and no wonder. When, later in the century, the stiff shirt collars and high coat collars shrank and coats loosened and trousers became straight and loose, men must have felt much freer. They still worried, however, about the hang of their trousers, automatically pulling them up before sitting down, to prevent bagging at the knee. This habit continues as long as men have a neat crease down the front of each trouser leg.

Late Nineteenth Century. This was about the time lounge suits were beginning to be worn. I always have the feeling that men's manners, at this time, varied considerably according to their company. You can imagine the almost visible change when the ladies left the room. Did this work both ways, I wonder?

As there were only small changes in fashion for so long there was less and less obvious class distinction in dress. So subtleties became more and more important. Cut and quality counted, of course, but money alone could buy them. There were also such things as the precise amount of linen shown, and the manner of knotting a tie—there was great variety in this, and those who knew doubtless looked at a man's tie before anything else. Such details would be of the first importance to mashers and knuts and other dandies.

Gentlemen still carried a stick or cane. So they had to be able to manage stick and gloves easily in one hand (no gentleman would be seen without gloves). You might even

80. 1841. Part of a *Punch* drawing showing Sir Robert Peel. There is nothing extreme in his appearance, not at waist, chest, shoulder nor collar. Note that he holds hat, cane and gloves.

have to touch your hat while holding a cane. What else can you do if you have a lady on your arm and meet another? For you must make a polite gesture of recognition, yet have no hand free to lift your hat in the usual way. Actors will find this can take quite a lot of practice.

By the turn of the century a little informality had begun to creep in, which meant an easier manner generally. Clothes were on the whole looser, freer and more shapeless, imposing less upon their wearers. Combinations had become an accepted article of underwear, and made life and movement more comfortable for those who wore them. That means your advanced, more modern man holds himself and moves slightly differently from the diehards for a plain physical reason as well as because of the difference in his personality.

Modern. The effect of the 1914–18 war on life and manners is a matter of social history. But since then men's underwear has become lighter and there is less of it, while their outer garments also became lighter and more comfortable—with a corresponding ease and freedom of movement. The habit of carrying a walking stick has gone out. Elderly men continued to carry one well into the nineteen-thirties and a short swagger cane was still part of an army officer's uniform during the Second World War.

Nowadays there is no expected high standard of carriage and deportment (except in the Forces and then only on parade), or even of behaviour to any great degree. The very lack of it is as distinctive, and often as deliberate, as the controlled grace of an earlier generation.

WOMEN

The nineteenth century saw more changes in women's clothes, and their corresponding movements, than almost any other. As Mrs. Grundy-like gentility became the thing, and the ideal of the "little woman" became popular,

81. Eighteen-fifties. The lady is neatly enveloped in her shawl.

women, like men, lost any flamboyance they had. A quiet, unobtrusive manner with small movements was the thing.

The century began with the free and flimsy Empire style. Then, as more and more petticoats were worn, skirts grew wider and quite short while waists tightened and slipped back to their natural position, with big puffed sleeves that enhanced the shape of the lower arm (1830). You might be constricted with stays to maintain that small waist, but the full rather short skirts left your legs free. The shape of your arm was nearly as important as the size of your waist, and playing an instrument at a musical evening was a good way to show it off. A young lady might even choose to play the harp rather than the piano simply because it was more effective in showing off her shapely arm. And now, for the first time since the Restoration, shoulders were to be seen, at least in evening dress. Another feature to be shown off if possible.

Big hats were fashionable, and elaborate coiffures for evening—both need a good carriage of the head, without which the wearer looks silly. Both hats and bonnets were worn during this century. Hats, on the whole, were the more dashing. The same person would wear both at different times according to the occasion, her mood, or the impression she wanted to make; so she would be likely to change her manner slightly to match. Servants would rarely be allowed to wear hats, and bonnet trimmings were frowned on for them too, as being too flighty. A bonnet can be a gay confection or a badge of service.

The correct, smart angle to wear a hat was constantly changing—straight, tilted, forward, sideways (which side?), back. If you are wearing nineteenth (or twentieth) century clothes, it is worth checking the correct angle to wear your hat with them, and then considering the attitude of the person concerned to high fashion. In Charlotte M. Yonge's *Daisy Chain* (1856), for instance, even the youngest of Dr. May's daughters would not dream of going out bareheaded

82. 1841. The shawl worn as a stole might have been worn thirty
or forty years earlier.

83. 1849. Another way to wear shawl or stole.

84. 1847. In evening dress, the lady's stole is worn solely as decoration.

or without gloves. The heroine, Edith, wore bonnets in her teens, and wore them so as to shade her face. Miss Yonge wrote as though the fashion of wearing a bonnet so that it seems to have slid right to the back of your head was objectionably fast. Now her family of gentlefolk lived in a small country town and were, to a modern taste, quite unbearably priggish; but her extremely popular book must have had some relation to reality, even if it were a little idealized. The point of this is that it shows how such small details as the angle of a bonnet change with each person's character and attitude as well as with their position in life; and how you can indicate these things by the way you wear your clothes.

For most of the nineteenth century, when your hat was off your cap was still on. Only children and young girls went bareheaded; matrons, spinsters "of a certain age" and servants all wore caps. They varied, of course, from those that quite covered the head to mere scraps of lace. As in the previous century there was great if subtle variety in caps—the ladies of Mrs. Gaskell's *Cranford* felt strongly about cap patterns. Propriety still required you to put something on your head. By the third quarter of the century, however, they began to be old-fashioned and by the eighteen-seventies were definitely so. Women were beginning to emancipate themselves in more ways than one.

Mid-century. Skirts soon dropped to the ground again, and ankles were officially hidden until the next century. In practice, of course, they were often glimpsed, by accident or design. But in days of official prudery the hiding or showing of ankles could be almost a minor art. In these conditions even the sight of a petticoat had an effect; there were definite fashions in petticoats—white, coloured, frilly, flounced, etc.! These are facts that wearers of these clothes must always remember, for the management of her skirts and petticoats illustrates a woman's whole character.

So does her way of wearing her shawl and bonnet,

85. 1862. Is it possible to come closer, in crinolines?

144

though maybe less plainly. Shawls varied in size; cashmere shawls were extremely expensive, but by the middle of the century good shawls were being manufactured in Britain. A large shawl could envelop a woman (as in Drawing 81) while the smaller one could be worn in nearly as many ways as a stole (see Drawings 82 and 83). The middle-class lady of Drawing 84 is wearing a stole with her evening dress.

Skirts got fuller and fuller, with more and heavier petticoats, until the invention of the steel crinoline must have come as a blessing. Before its arrival the really smart woman could not wear less than eight petticoats under her dress. Some of them were padded and otherwise thickened, and others flounced, to add to the final effect. The weight was considerable, and you had to walk in short glides to be at all graceful. The hoop was much easier to carry, although its very lightness created difficulties and it was impossible for two women wearing crinolines to come really close to each other (see Drawing 85). Remember when wearing it that the greatest width is at the bottom. When you wear a farthingale it does not matter how much you walk into things (below waist level, anyway), your skirts ripple and stay decent. You can't do the same in a crinoline. Neither can you bend too far forward. The lady in Drawing 86 is leaning as far forward as is reasonable and safe; it is the angle of her body that does most to give her that "typical" look of her period. If you really want to get low down you must bend both knees and squat.

Yet women went for walks in crinolines, and even climbed stiles. To walk safely in a crinoline you mustn't take risks; no violent movements, care over the amount of tilt you allow—and send gentlemen first over stiles—these are the main precautions. They were soon habits to women who lived in crinolines. By 1860 women of all classes were wearing them, which meant they knew how to walk in them safely and decently. (There was for a time a fashion for looping up your dress a little above your petticoat to go out walking.

86. 1849. Is it safe to bend farther forward?

87. Eighteen-eighties. A smart lady with the hollow-backed posture inseparable from her bustle and long stays.

88. 1887. A serious-minded young woman; but she has the same posture, for the same reasons, as the lady of Drawing 87.

This influenced the style of walking dresses.) There was no variation in the height of the hem for working women, such as sometimes happened in the eighteenth century. Taking society as a whole, instead of just the upper classes, the women of the time must have had better deportment than the men.

When the crinoline shrank, women's stays tended to be less rigid than before. This was perhaps because elastic was now in use, but more probably because a voluptuous look was fashionable.

In 1877 combinations were first worn; at the time they were a great relief after so many complicated underclothes. And in 1878 suspenders began to replace garters, a further relief. As the crinoline went out of fashion more petticoats were needed, but they were thinner and flimsier than before. That means you have to allow for them when walking, but you don't have a great weight to support.

At this time, and officially still today, the "marks of a lady" are her gloves, handkerchief and shoes. Readers of *Little Women* will remember Jo's distress when she had no clean gloves for the dance—a worse disgrace than her scorched dress; Meg's delight in a well-filled glove box; and Marmee's "Girls, girls! *have* you both got nice pocket-handkerchiefs?" These details meant more than money in terms of social position. In the same way, a line was clearly drawn between married and unmarried women. Age had nothing to do with it; the latter was not expected to put herself forward, while the former had a position in the world. So as soon as a girl was married she was likely to dress like a matron, which must have looked incongruous at times.

Late Nineteenth Century. Let us return to the wearing of clothes. The long-bodied bustle of the eighteen-eighties involved wearing long stays. You stood with a hollow back (as in Drawings 87 and 88) and your head well up. Even a blue-stocking who went in for simple clothes (like the girl in

89. Late Eighteen-nineties. With her skirt gathered correctly in one hand this lady can, with no inconvenience, wear a walking dress with a very full, long skirt.

Drawing 88—ideas of simplicity change) had a big bustle and the hollow back that went with it. Remember to hold the bustle itself well out of the way as you sit down; you do this with the angle of your behind, and hands are no help. You can't sit well back in a chair, either. With a dress tight to the knees tiny steps are a necessity; and walk from the knee, for wiggling hips are definitely out.

Wearers of the Rational Dress, of course, moved with a conscious freedom which included some exaggeration. But early training in deportment would have left its mark on them too.

By 1890 the bustle had gone and the hour-glass figure was in fashion. This is the famous Gibson Girl, and many women needed to pad hips or bosom to get the right effect. It was the fashion to wear a lot of flounced petticoats, flounces and frills and frou-frou under your smooth skirt (the same idea as the can-can dress, only much more genteel of course). You walked with your skirts held up at one side (see Part I and Drawings 4, 5 and 89)—not too high, though—and could give a delightful glimpse of those intriguing frills if you wished, showing a little to imply a lot more. But remember that it was immodest to show any leg, although those skirts that trailed on the ground had to be brushed and sponged clean after every wearing. To make this easier it was a common practice to put an edging of some coarse, easily cleaned braid on one's skirt. A rich woman with a maid would probably not bother but it made life much easier for the ordinary working woman. As she walked she would take great pains to keep her skirt as clear of the ground as she decently could, to save herself work later.

Twentieth Century. At the beginning of the twentieth century hips were minimized as much as possible. You wore corsets that were long below the waist, with stocking suspenders fastened to them. Your dress was smooth over your tightly corseted hips, but from the knee down those petticoats were a mass of frills—you can hardly control

90. 1901. This smart lady shows the particular stance of the period, with bust thrown forward and seat thrown back. It was not yet usual to roll umbrellas and parasols into a tight stick.

91. 1901. Part of a *Punch* drawing. A middle-class housewife, who now follows fashion closely enough (and wears similar shaped corsets) to have the same posture as the very fashionable ladies of Drawings 90 and 92.

153

92. 1901. Part of a *Punch* drawing. Another view of the same
attributes.

them with your hands, so don't try. The breasts were pushed together and forward in a single mass, while you held your shoulders down. (Bust bodices, which turned into the brassière, came in at this time and saved a lot of strain and fruitless attempts to avoid an ugly wobble.) Your only possible stance, which of course became fashionable, was swaying slightly forward. The ladies in Figures 90 and 92 are dressed in the height of fashion, and hold themselves in as extreme a form of this posture as they can. But Figure 91 is an ordinary middle-class housewife and there is surprisingly little difference between her stance and theirs.

Dog-collar necklaces were fashionable, which means that long necks were thought beautiful—so make your neck as long as possible. You can alter at least its apparent length slightly by the angle of your head.

The next important fashion, about 1911, was for a straight and narrow line topped by a huge hat, which just required its wearer to stand straight (see Drawing 93). But the one after, for hobble skirts, forced you to walk from the knees again. Keep as still as you can above the knees; it is dangerously easy to produce a vulgar wriggle in this dress. It was incredibly inconvenient for daily life, with buses and trains, and for more or less emancipated women fighting for the vote, and was only worn by women who particularly wanted to look smart (see Drawing 94). These tight dresses cut down the possible number of undergarments, anyway. It is worth commenting that this was the first time that fashion made women wear skirts too *tight* for ease.

Modern. Before and during the 1914–18 war underclothes became fewer and less restricting, and clothes became something like those we wear today (see Figures 95 and 96). During the war several inches of leg were shown, with a corresponding freedom of movement. Ideas of decency were changing, which naturally affected manners—it was

93. 1911. A straight line with a narrow skirt; she must hold herself very straight. The big hat, wider than her shoulders, imposes a good carriage.

possible for a woman to cross her legs in public as a matter of course.

In the years after that war skirt lengths changed a great

94. 1913. Part of a *Punch* drawing. Hobble skirts really impeded movement and made it dangerously easy to move vulgarly.

deal, moving up and down; while clothes continued to be modern in style, even casual (see Drawings 97 and 98). They are still "feminine" though, unlike what was to appear within a decade. In this decade a woman's style of dress (within fashion, of course) and her manner of behaving, moving, etc., changed quickly, together. And women were free to cover a greater range than ever before without

95. 1916. Part of a *Punch* drawing. A short skirt and comfortable
clothes; easy to wear.

96. 1916. Part of a *Punch* drawing. A short skirt and no constriction. Shoe styles matter, and ankles are ceasing to be
exciting.

97. 1921. Part of a *Punch* drawing. Skirts have crept higher and there is more casualness.

98. 1921. Part of a *Punch* drawing. The elegant woman still holds herself very well.

being ostracized. The girl who, in 1921, can calmly recline on a sofa in public with her skirt rucked up above her knees (Drawing 99) demonstrates the changed climate of opinion.

During the nineteen-twenties make-up came into more general use than ever before, being now quite respectable. Modern methods produced cosmetics that would not harm

99. 1921. Part of a *Punch* drawing. It is not indecent to show your legs, even up to the knee, in public.

the wearer, which may have had something to do with the changed attitude—whatever the principle of the thing, there was no more physical danger involved. But that alone could not account for the changed attitude; a young woman would now openly attend to her make-up in public!

With the short, bare-armed clothes of the late nineteen-twenties, and the fashionable lack of shape, women had more freedom than ever before. You could throw yourself about, take great strides, and cross your legs. And you did. Underclothes were fewer and less constricting than ever, too. As ideals of deportment vanished you could see women standing, rather knock-kneed, with their weight

100. 1928. Part of a *Punch* drawing. An ordinary girl, bare-armed in the street; she has her weight thrown to one side and her hip thrust out.

101. 1928. Part of a *Punch* drawing. A "typical" posture; almost knock-kneed with the weight on one leg and a hip thrust out.

on one leg and a hip thrown out uglily to advertise the fact (see Drawings 100 and 101). Another odd posture which was seen then, and which we still tend to use, especially when wearing short, tight skirts, is shown in Drawing 102. It is ugly but often feels rather sophisticated—the knees sag, the behind is pushed out and the body bent forward in a straight line to the shoulders. There are only two things you can then do with your head; either poke it forward or throw it back.

During the 1939–45 war and the years since the same trend has continued in both sexes. Clothes and under-clothing are light and unrestricting. We are not usually trained in good deportment as children, nor is it held up to us as something to aim at. The result is that we sag and loll about, gestures tend to be uncontrolled yet small, and there is less and less distinction between the walk of a man and that of a woman.

So the actor who has been working on the carriage and deportment of another age must consciously change back when in modern dress. Small steps and a smooth floating gait look right in any woman's dress except today's. In today's they look plain silly. The correct "period" walk for today is, in fact, the opposite of almost every other. Men sag and show an undisciplined shapelessness of posture and demeanour. Yet their clothes are getting gayer, and seem designed to show off the masculine shape to greater advantage than any since they stopped wearing skin-tight pantaloons; some might say since the fifteenth century. Women also show this undisciplined casualness—we cross our legs in public and walk from the hips with steps as big as a man's (unless wearing too high heels). There is just one situation in which women still walk from the knee—when wearing a tight skirt that allows no choice. But the modern girl doesn't know how to do it and moves awkwardly, with a sort of twist and trot. No pre-1914 woman would have

102. 1928. Part of a *Punch* drawing. A posture that still goes with short tight skirts (the clutch-coat emphasizes it), with the behind pushed out and shoulders forward.

moved like that, but then there is no precedent for that short, tight skirt.

There never was a time when everybody behaved perfectly, according to the ideas of that time. But in the same way that the spirit of each age shows in its literature, furniture, fashions and other social manifestations, so it shows in the manner and the manners of the people of the age. General behaviour must be in key with the rest or you have only fancy-dress unreality, while correct demeanour makes the whole picture truthful—and convincing. Such knowledge also gives us a deeper understanding of the people of other times; and it gives the actor not only ease and comfort but, together with his producer, a subtle and flexible tool.

Index

(Figures in italics refer to the illustrations)

8544